BLADE® PRESENTS

44th Edition

Knives

The World's Greatest Knife Book

2024

EDITED BY
JOE KERTZMAN

Published by

Gun Digest® Books, an imprint of Caribou Media Group, LLC
Gun Digest Media
5583 W. Waterford Ln., Suite D
Appleton WI 54913
gundigest.com

To order books or other products call 920.471.4522 ext. 104
or visit us online at gundigeststore.com

CAUTION: Technical data presented here, particularly technical data on handloading and on firearms adjustment and alteration, inevitably reflects individual experience with particular equipment and components under specific circumstances the reader cannot duplicate exactly. Such data presentations therefore should be used for guidance only and with caution. Caribou Media accepts no responsibility for results obtained using these data.

ISBN: 978-1-959265-00-9

Edited by Joe Kertzman and Corey Graff
Designed by Joey Meyers
Cover design by Gene Coo

Printed in China

10 9 8 7 6 5 4 3 2 1

Dedication and Acknowledgments

I t seems like I always remember the hands. I can picture my dad's hands clear as day, holding the red Swiss Army Knife (SAK) retrieved from his front pants pocket. Dad used that knife to cut slices of apples and share them with me. He cut rope with it for makeshift clotheslines on our many family camping trips over the years. The SAK stripped wire insulation and cut loose threads from his and my shirts. Dad had long, thin, white hands with big knuckle pads. He was the gentlest, kindest, smartest man I have ever known.

Dad wasn't a handyman, but if something needed fixing, he could do it. He was a slow and methodical guy who thought projects out long before tackling them. I remember him using the pocketknife to sharpen one of several pencils on his workbench and draw out plans for whatever he was working on. All the pencils had blade marks—there was no pencil sharpener on that old wooden bench with a vise at the end.

Over the 19 years that I worked as the associate editor of *BLADE Magazine*, I accumulated a few two- and three-blade stag-handle pocketknives with blade etchings marking anniversaries of Gun Digest, a sister publication produced by the same publishing company. I gave one of those knives to Dad and he cherished it. I remember talking him into going to a rock concert with me at Summerfest in Milwaukee, and poor Dad had to walk the knife back to the car when the metal detector sounded off at the gate.

When Alzheimer's disease started to take its hold on him, he'd make up a mnemonic device or saying where the first letter of each word would remind him of all of the things he needed to carry with him before leaving the house. I have no idea what the saying was, but "k" was one of the letters starting a word and reminding him to bring his knife.

When my son was little, I taught him how to use a knife properly. He also had instruction from his Boy Scout master when earning the whittling badge. Once Danny had the hang of safe cutting and slicing, I gave him a few of the folders I had bought on the cheap at knife shows and flea markets. I made him promise not to take them to school and explained what could happen if he did. I told him he could bring whatever knife he wanted when we went camping.

During a family vacation to Florida, while going through airport security, I noticed the TSA agent sweating over my son's carry-on bag, going through every pocket as if he knew there was something there, but he couldn't find it. I asked, "Danny, do you have something in your bag?" He looked at me with his big browns and said, "Dad, you told me I could take my knife camping." I said, "Don't worry, bud, just show the man where it is."

He did, and when the TSA agent pulled it out of an inside pocket in my son's bag, my heart sank. It was a big, black assisted-opening folder with a wicked-looking tanto blade. The agent pushed the thumb stud, and that blade flew open with a *thwack*! He looked at me, laid the knife down on a ruler, and said, "You're a quarter inch from going to jail. What do you want me to do with the knife?" I replied, "It's yours. Keep it or throw it away." My son looked at me with tears in his eyes, and I said, "Don't worry, Danny, I'll buy you a new one."

I'm lucky to have an extremely supportive wife, so when I made editing a knife magazine into a career, she enthusiastically accumulated her own collection of blades. A horse lover and owner, she had one of the bladesmiths at a knife show pound out a hoof pick for her, and she keeps a folder and fixed blade in a suede leather pouch in the barn for cutting string off hay bales, opening feed, and countless other chores. She squirreled a few of the nicer knives she took possession of in her top dresser drawer where they remain to this day.

It's good to have a supportive family, and I acknowledge them and dedicate this 44ᵗʰ edition of the *KNIVES* book to my mom and dad, Jack, and Cathy Kertzman; my wife, Tricia; and son and daughter, Danny, and Cora. Thank you for keeping memories alive for me. □

~ Joe Kertzman

Contents

On The Cover

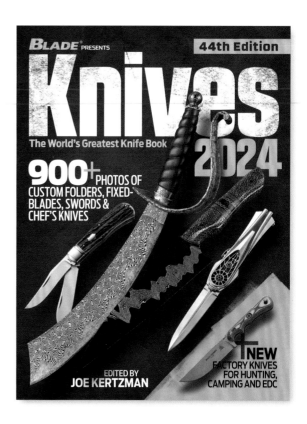

The *KNIVES 2024* cover offers a knife for every taste, starting with Jim Dunlap's two-blade model at left, this in hollow-ground CPM 154 steel, stainless hardware, and amber jigged-bone handle scales. Swooping down from top to bottom is a David Lisch pirate sword defined by a "Tribal Dreams" mosaic damascus blade with an "Ocean Waves" edge wrap, a wrought iron guard awash in melted gold, and a carved Mexican kingwood handle. Directly beneath it rests a Justin Lyman chef's knife sporting a Baker Forge & Tool "Dark Mai" blade and a handle assembled from five kinds of Micarta. The all-steel Corrado Moro "Huayra" art folder is a carved and sculpted beauty inlaid with precious gemstones on one of the two exposed gears within the bolster. At the bottom-right is a handy TOPS Knives Muley Skinner designed by Leo Espinoza and featuring a flat-ground, stonewashed 154CM blade, a black-and-tan G-10 handle, and orange liners. It comes in a Kydex sheath. With so many quality knives to choose from, perhaps a collection is in order. *(SharpByCoop photos of the handmade knives)*

Introduction

They touch so many lives. Tell someone you are a knifemaker, that you work for a production knife company, collect handmade or factory knives, make a living purveying or dealing in blades of all kinds, or are an editor of the *KNIVES* annual book, and the conversation inevitably flows. Perhaps when mentioning such an occupation or hobby, you get an odd look or two, but whether the person you're engaging with truly engages or not, someone nearby likely will. It happens all the time. Knives touch so many lives.

Maybe you'll receive questions about what the ideal kitchen or hunting knife is, how to sharpen a blade, or the best way to choose a quality pocketknife. Often, someone within earshot has tried their hand at making knives or knows someone who builds them. Folks often have stories about their favorite knives or ones their dad, uncle, or grandpa carried. Still others recall watching their grandma use her paring or butcher knife daily in the garden, kitchen, and around the home.

As much as many despise the mass media, it has helped bring awareness to handmade blades and quality factory tools. One would have to live under a rock not to have heard of The History Channel television show "Forged in Fire" and spinoffs such as "Forged in Fire: Knife or Death" and "Forged in Fire: Beat the Judges." The BLADE Show in Atlanta has been successful in bringing the BladeSports International Cutting World Championships and Blade HQ Balisong Competition to a mass audience.

Of all TV Networks, CBS has been good to the knifemaking craft in recent years (negative press aside, and there's plenty of it.) Nearly 15 years ago, CBS correspondent Scott Pelley did a full-blown feature story on Michael O'Machearley, a knifemaker from Wilmington, Ohio, who lost his job when the local DHL hub employing 8,000 workers shut down. O'Machearley, who had been a part-time knifemaker, turned to his craft full-time to pay the bills. It wasn't the first tragedy that the knifemaker had faced head-on, with him and his wife having tragically lost their oldest son when he was shot down in a helicopter and killed alongside 16 other Marines in Iraq.

More recently, my wife and I quickly hit "rewind" on the TV when we saw that Murray Carter was being featured on "CBS Saturday Morning," February 4, 2023. Carter, who spent nearly two decades in Japan before bringing eastern bladesmithing techniques west, revealed some of his best knifemaking secrets during the program. A 17th-generation Yoshimoto bladesmith, Carter's kitchen knives are works of art and exceptional forged tools. Watching the episode brought back a flood of memories of Carter standing behind his BLADE Show and BLADE Show West booths sharpening knives and encouraging anyone who stopped by to try their hand at honing a blade. Sure enough, during the CBS episode, Carter was shown wearing a shirt that said "Stop Vegetable Abuse. Use Sharp Knives." It made me proud to have known and interviewed Carter in the past, and to be a part of the knife industry in general.

The feature articles in *KNIVES 2024* bring the knifemaking craft to an international audience. Some of the best knife writers in the world have penned articles herein on everything from Eastern European knifemakers offering value-priced knives to polishing Japanese swords and "The Kitchen Knife as a Survival Blade," "Where Tacticals Got Their Edges," "Rescue Knives Save Lives," and "Hot Handle Materials Include Hybrids." Respected knifemaker Tim Zowada gives tips on precision layout and measurement when building handmade blades, attorney Evan F. Nappen unveils his collection of special edition Randall knives, and bladesmith/tomahawk maker Ryan Johnson reveals who he believes makes up the trifecta of master knifemaking craftsmen.

Identifying "Trends" has always been a major selling point of the *KNIVES* annual book, and trending today are styles we cover in an "Abundance of Bog Oak," "Money Micarta," "Clinch Pick, Utility & EDC Knives," "Harpoon-Style Blades," "Boujee Bowies," "Crème de la Crème Chef's Knives, "Fashionable Flippers," and much more. "State of the Art" categories include "Scrimshaw Sans Flaw," "Wood & Resin Fusion," "Dyed in the Wood Practitioners," "Copper Showstoppers," "Clad-to-the-Core Steel," and "Edgy Ladder Patterns." The custom knives herein incorporate mosaic damascus, engraving, jewel inlay and engraving, carving, "Golden Touches," and "Sculpted Features."

Combine all that with the Factory Trends and Knifemaker Directory sections of the book, and *KNIVES 2024* puts into high gear the concept of knives touching so many lives. I know they touch yours and mine! □

~ Joe Kertzman

WOODEN SWORD AWARD

This is the first time in 44 years of the *KNIVES* Annual book that the Wooden Sword Award is being presented posthumously, but it seems to make sense in this case, as the handmade sword being recognized has stood the test of time.

Swords with storied histories, particularly ones this beautiful, are worth spending some time with. The "Michael's Sword" designed by the late Hugh Bartrug was reproduced by Darrel Ralph as a commissioned piece by a doctor that Hugh knew. Darrel passed away, in 2021, after complications from a stroke. Oddly, his friend had also suffered a stroke.

"Hugh and I were good friends for many years," Darrel Ralph said in a July 2005 Bladeforums post. "He had a stroke that left him unable to make knives several years ago. The doctor asked Hugh who could make him a sword that was similar to Hugh's original."

"Hugh gave him some names, and the doctor asked me to do the project," Ralph remembered at the time. "My rendition of the sword that Hugh made took eight months of about four hours a day to make. It has a twisted damascus center core with an O1 band forge welded around the edge. The fittings are 18-karat gold that I cast or made. The blade exhibits bas relief work and was 24k-gold plated after etching."

"It was a great honor to be asked to build this sword with Hugh's blessing and recommendation," Ralph said in his 2005 post. "It was also a very large undertaking! Hugh was a great man. He made many masterpieces that are in collections all over the world."

With gold lettering and gold leaf work, the piece is based on a theme from Dante's "Inferno" and inscribed with passages from "Inferno." The octagonal handle has mother-of-pearl panels, and the tip of the pommel features a gold-lip pearl inlay.

Having been reacquired by the maker at least once in his lifetime, the sword has been in more than one collection. At the time of the editor awarding Darrel Ralph with a much belated and deserved 2024 Wooden Sword Award for the Michael's Sword, it was for sale on the Quintessential Cutlery website, www.quintcut.com, for a cool $28,000. Beautiful work, Darrel, and you were also a great man like your friend, Hugh. □

~ Joe Kertzman

True Masters Of Their Craft

The author holds a Q&A session with his "fantasy trio team" of knifemakers.

By Ryan Johnson, RMJ Tactical, rmjtactical.com

o be called a master of a craft centuries ago was no small thing. Often apprenticeships started in childhood, the child living with the master's family and working simply for room, board, and his education in the craft.

In a forging shop, this meant building and tending fires, swinging a sledgehammer as a *striker*, and doing general finish work. By tending the irons in the fire and striking, the apprentice watched the master work through different projects and solve problems, learning the process and secrets of forging iron and steel.

Working for years, the apprentice became a journeyman, forging on his own but still in the master's shop and under his scrutiny. Some never progressed past the journeyman rank, but a few were skilled enough to become masters. In some guilds, the apprentices had to pass tests, proving their skill.

I used to have people ask me as a young man if I was a master bladesmith. Having worked with several real masters, my response was always, "I've not even lived long enough to become a master yet."

The gentlemen I was privileged enough to interview for this article are all masters. Yes, they are master smiths in the American Bladesmith Society (ABS), but more than that, each is a true master of his craft.

They have stood the test of time, and their knives have as well. They've been in the business long enough to remember the BLADE Show moving to Atlanta, and their blades are still in high demand today. I thought it would be interesting to get their perspectives on the knifemaking world, both then and now. It is interesting to see how these makers influenced each other over the years. I believe their thoughts are worth our time.

When did you start making knives? What was the knifemaking world like back then, and what is it like in your eyes now?

Daniel Winkler:

I started making knives in high school, in 1974. The first knife I made is on display in the Winkler Knives Actual Museum. Attached to it is a document that details the transitions I made in knifemaking. When I first started, I had no idea there were others making knives.

Steve Schwarzer was my first contact with a real knifemaker/bladesmith. I met him at the Southeastern NMLRA (National Muzzle Loading Rifle Association) Rendezvous. I started making knives for reenactments and customers who liked the buck skinner way of life. Steve opened my eyes to the custom knife world.

In 1988, my longtime partner, wife, and sheath maker, Karen, and I went full-time into making knives and related accessories. I would hate to be starting a career making knives now. The ABS and other individuals and organizations have done a great job teaching people how to make a knife. No one is teaching anyone how to sell a knife. It's hard to build

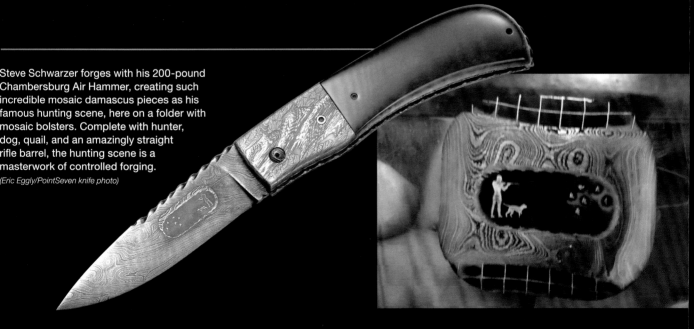

Steve Schwarzer forges with his 200-pound Chambersburg Air Hammer, creating such incredible mosaic damascus pieces as his famous hunting scene, here on a folder with mosaic bolsters. Complete with hunter, dog, quail, and an amazingly straight rifle barrel, the hunting scene is a masterwork of controlled forging.
(Eric Eggly/PointSeven knife photo)

name recognition, and without that, it would be tough to be a true full-time maker with no other source of income. It was tough back in the late 1980s and '90s.

Now, with social media and self-promotion, anyone can claim to be anything. It seems "he who knows algorithms has the edge" over those who know how to make a quality knife. Knife shows used to be where a maker made a name for himself as well as how he dealt with customers. There are makers now who show pictures taken from my website to sell their knives and axes.

Jason Knight:

I started making knives in 1989 and entered the community as a full-time maker in 2001. It was the golden age of knifemaking. It was a much smaller world back then. Everyone knew which makers were setting standards, influencing trends, and creating innovative designs. Though the community was much smaller, the resources for learning were scarce, at least they seemed to be to a teen in rural South Carolina.

I read *BLADE Magazine* a lot in those days. George Heron, Daniel Winkler, and a maker out of Walterboro, South Carolina, were my only direct contacts with knifemakers until I attended my first BLADE Show in 1995. The knifemaking world has experienced enormous growth in recent years. Skilled makers are more open to teaching their craft today in both the stock-removal and bladesmithing/forging genres of blade making.

Steve Schwarzer:

I started in the late '60s. I made a few knives I call "knife-shaped objects" because I did not understand heat-treating, which I consider to be the heart of the blade. I began forging in 1972 after reading a book by Alex Bealer. There was a page-and-a-half on forging

World famous for his blade-making skills, Jason Knight fashioned this composite twist-damascus beauty with titanium fittings and a desert ironwood handle. Note how the damascus pattern flows with the forged tip and how the handle complements the blade shape. *(Caleb Royer photo)*

knives. It set a fire that never went out.

What was the knifemaking world like back then? It was isolated with little available knowledge. There were very few makers that I knew of until I finally found a knowledgeable maker in Jacksonville, Florida. His name is Bobby Tison. He helped by introducing me to the beginnings of what is modern knifemaking. He specialized in folding knives and graciously shared his hard-earned knowledge with me.

I started out forging and connected with some local blacksmiths. I began reading what little was available on knifemaking, and it was an eye-opener. I began to seek out other makers. I had read about damascus steel, and after several attempts at forging it, I knew I needed help. I contacted Alfred Pendray in Williston, Florida. He agreed to show me his method after traveling to his shop. I met with his dad, John Pendray. Mr. John spent a half-day showing me the method. I came home and the rest is history.

There were some great makers in the Northeast. Alfred and I traveled to New York to meet with them and others in the late '70s early '80s. Among them were Jim Schmidt, Don Fogg, and Jimmy Fikes. These men became my guiding light, along with Daryl Meier, whom I consider my greatest teacher and inspiration.

(The knifemaking world now) It is amazing, embodying a transformation from no information to all information. LOL. There was no internet. Hi-tech was a fax machine. Today's knifemaking world is a fantasyland of technical expertise and talent. There are so many new makers with huge talent, they're hard to count. I love hanging out with these young wizards. I have learned that there is not enough time to study everything I want to know. I am still exploring, making knives, and developing techniques that I share by teaching.

In 1988, Daniel Winkler and his longtime partner, wife, and sheath maker, Karen, went full-time into making knives and related accessories. The Winkler Knives RnD Axe Series is a collaborative design between Winkler and skilled Sayoc Kali martial arts trainer, Rafael Kayanan. The full-size model is a favorite among operators and servicemen who choose their own equipment. The handle design provides a standard grip position, as well as a secondary close-quarter grip that was developed to emulate the feel of a handgun.

What were your big influences back then? What influences your work now?

Winkler:

My influences from the late 1980s to around 2010 came from early American and American Indian history. I looked at all the other makers' work and tried to evaluate how I could use their design and execution talents to better my work. I could see a little something that would give me an idea on how to use a texture, design flow, or material within my own design parameters. Now, as back then, I look to high-performance knives and axes for design and process influences. "Form follows function" is a true statement.

Knight:

Old cars from the '50s, like '57 Chevys, art lines and curves, and the outdoors influenced my designs early on. Growing up in a swamp also created the need for specific types of knives that I couldn't find, so I had to make them myself—the idea of making a better knife. I had not seen the designs I wanted, so I worked hard to develop my style early on. Today, I get inspiration from subtle details that make the knives more interesting, and from ancient traditions kept alive by bladesmiths like Yoshindo Yoshihara.

Schwarzer:

(Then) Daryl Meier, Jim Schmidt, Don Fogg, and Jimmy Fikes were my influences. (Now) I am influenced by new talent through my teaching and sharing techniques with very talented young people. I've also always loved technology. I like to apply those techniques to my work.

How has your philosophy as a maker changed over the years?

Winkler:

Early on, I made knives and axes for the buckskinner crowd. Then, my customers were users/collectors. Now, the customers are more real-world users with some collectors coming on board. My true philosophy has and still is to make a knife or axe that does not fail in the field and that looks good, too.

Knight:

My first 10 years of knifemaking were spent focusing on custom knives and learning how to make them. Being a full-time knifemaker during the difficult years of 2009-2012 led me to become more resourceful and experimental with other materials. Today, I want the most direct way to get to the next level. As a perpetual student, I seek it out for myself, and as an effective teacher, I share it with my students.

Schwarzer:

My absolutes have softened, but my drive to achieve has not. I was a traditionalist. I have learned to accept any technology that will improve my work. I'll respond to anyone who says, "That is not traditional" by saying, "I can make my tools from raw ore; Can you?"

How has that change affected your knives and process?

Knight:

I developed and refined my teaching techniques and expanded my knowledge-sharing through online courses. By experimenting with forging techniques, I can forge to finish, leaving minimal grinding needed.

Steve Schwarzer shows off his mosaic damascus BLADE Show logo (toward the heel of the blade) at the World's Largest Knife Show, in Atlanta. Steve usually has a line of folks at shows waiting for a chance to meet and talk with him

Jason Knight is known for forging pieces like this high-density, random-pattern damascus bowie with titanium and copper fittings. The polished ivory contrasts nicely with the patterned steel. *(SharpByCoop knife photo)*

I have also recently begun to explore manufacturing processes; this influence comes directly from Winkler Knives and RMJ Tactical.

Schwarzer:

It has literally made my work what it is. Adapting machinery and techniques to my work drives everything I make. I have a shop full of tools and machines. Some I use. others not, but I thought they would be useful. LOL. If I can use a technique, I will use it to improve my work. If there's a machine or a tool that will improve my work that I can afford, I will own one.

Name three of your favorite makers when starting out. Has that list changed?

Winkler:

Steve Schwarzer, Don Fogg, and George Herron. Steve for processes and machine knowledge, Don for design flow, and George for business practices. Realistically, they all excel in design. Don just took a different path in materials and textures. Now I would have to add Jason Knight and Ryan Johnson. Both follow their own path, which is enlightening in this world of copy artists.

Knight:

In my early days, the makers who had the most significant influence on me were George Heron and Daniel Winkler. George was from South Carolina and was the first to encourage me to seek my path as a maker. I first met Daniel when I was in high school at the Wildlife Expo in Charleston. His frontier-style knives and especially his tomahawks profoundly influenced me. Every year I would bring a knife or warclub to show him. He was much more subtle with his thoughts than George, but those annual encounters eventually evolved into a lifelong friendship.

I also really liked what Steve Schwarzer was doing. I wrote a paper about his forging pictures in damascus for a high school English class. This list has stayed the same, but I have added to it. Jay Hendrickson taught me how to forge when I attended the Bill Moran School of Bladesmithing, in 2001. Jim Rodebaugh was my classmate during the Intro course and shared a lot of techniques for finishing knives. When I was working on my ABS master smith knives, I received a lot of encouragement from Jim Crowell to continue to push forward.

Schwarzer:

Starting out, it was Daryl Meier, Jim Schmidt, and

The primary uses for the Winkler Knives Drop Point Crusher models shown here are in combat and breaching operations. The overall balance of the handle to the blade encourages the user to get into the cut, with the thumb ramp adding extra power to heavy cutting.

Alfred Pendray. Now the list is longer.

Name three makers whose work you follow and why.

Winkler:

Jason Knight, Ryan Johnson, and W.R. Case & Sons. Jason because I have known him for a long time and he has set a recognizable style. Ryan because he creates his own designs in a manufacturing setting, and from all I have heard, has a great reputation in the field. W.R. Case because they have a connection with Winkler Knives with the American Heroes Series.

Knight:

My children, Tigerlily and Tristen, are the makers I follow most closely now. They are in that stage where they have mastered some of the materials. Both are skilled at forging and grinding. It is always interesting to see what they will come up with next. Another maker whose work I follow is Charlie Ellis. He is working on interesting patterns and knife concepts. He made a Boba Fett knife. I wanted it bad, but he made it as a gift for his friend.

Schwarzer:

There are too many to list, but at the top of that list, these makers are there. Henning Wilkinson's

work is exceptional in all fields, from design execution to material development. His knives tell a story, and he is an excellent writer of that story. Plus, he is a decent human being. Salem Straube is on this list because I consider him one of the most talented new pattern-weld designers that exist. His ability to design and execute damascus patterns is extraordinary, and his work speaks for itself. His ability to weave the material and execute the construction of his knives is just on a higher level.

I picked Joshua Prince because I know how he works and where he works. I am totally amazed at the art he produces using minimal tools. His pattern work is what draws me in. He's done some amazing things with simple tools.

I could easily add another dozen new makers to this list. The work being done today by many new makers is beyond extraordinary. I am honored both as a teacher and maker to be able to spend time and work with these amazing young people.

What advice would you offer to folks starting out making knives?

Winkler:

Keep it as a part-time/retirement business. A part-time activity can really be rewarding and provide extra money for expansion. Having to rely on selling products that are so widely available can take the fun out of being a knifemaker. Realistically, living expenses are high and a maker must do all the things to be successful. Make a product people want more than the other 10,000 makers, be a good bookkeeper so you know what it costs to make a knife for profit, be an accountant so Uncle Sam doesn't take everything you have, and pay for all kinds of insurance so a one-time incident doesn't ruin you.

Knight:

Find a teacher you really like and take some classes. There are many masters of the craft who are willing to share their knowledge. The cost of lessons to learn directly from a skilled teacher is far cheaper than the hours and price of learning by trial and error. Classes are also a great way to experience different kinds of equipment. Don't buy a bunch of things you don't need.

Schwarzer:

Keep your day job. If you're not going to make knives because you love it, then do something else. If you're just gonna dabble because it's interesting, keep it a hobby. It's hot, hard work and there's no "get by" factor. Do your best and improve each knife as your skills improve. Take lessons and the skills you need from a competent instructor.

What advice would you offer to folks just starting to enter the knife enthusiast world?

Knight:

Take the time to get to know the maker. Find out who the original influencers of the styles or elements you like are. Be a student of the styles you like. Don't buy anything because someone says it will be worth money in the future; buy it because you like it.

What will your legacy as a maker be?

Winkler:

I don't know. Karen and I have our family working for Winkler Knives and our hope is that they can continue when we both slow down and are gone. We have two main goals—to provide high-performance functional and quality tools for those who really use them, and to provide meaningful lasting jobs for good people. I think the next generation at Winkler Knives understands.

Knight:

I believe we are all created by a creator god to be makers, so my students are part of my legacy. Bladesmithing is difficult. I have shared designs and forging techniques that have influenced the industry for over 20 years. Through teaching, I inspire makers to level up their bladesmithing and provide a challenging experience to encourage everyday people to become makers.

Schwarzer:

My students will be my major legacy. The techniques I developed changed the way mosaic damascus is made and pattern-welding in general. I love the discovery of different methods and the adaptation of old methods. Hopefully, my friends and other makers who I have associated with come away feeling that I've added something to their lives.

Conclusion

It has been my honor to know these makers for decades. Like hundreds of others, I've learned important lessons and techniques from each of them. For me, their legacies will be making the knife world a better, more interesting place than when they found it. □

While pioneering mosaic damascus is what Steve Schwarzer (right) is known for, mentoring talented new bladesmiths will undoubtedly be his legacy.

EASTERN EUROPEAN MAKERS OFFERING
Value-Priced Knives

An overinflated market for forged blades at home caused the author to look elsewhere.

By Les Robertson

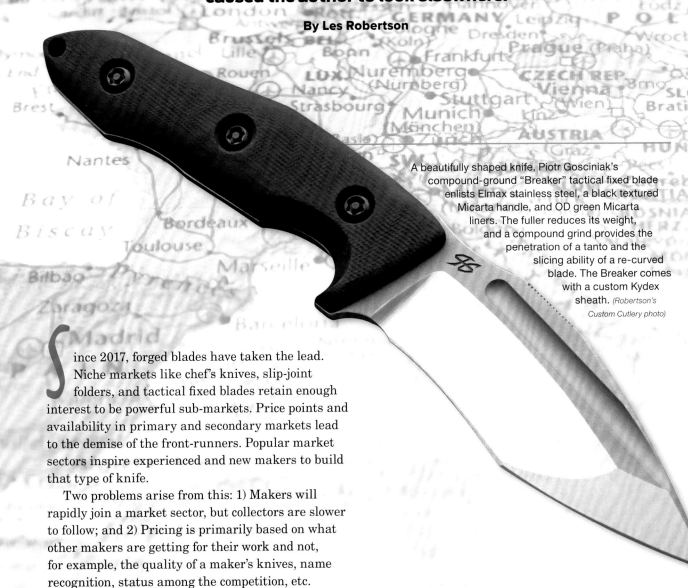

A beautifully shaped knife, Piotr Gosciniak's compound-ground "Breaker" tactical fixed blade enlists Elmax stainless steel, a black textured Micarta handle, and OD green Micarta liners. The fuller reduces its weight, and a compound grind provides the penetration of a tanto and the slicing ability of a re-curved blade. The Breaker comes with a custom Kydex sheath. *(Robertson's Custom Cutlery photo)*

Since 2017, forged blades have taken the lead. Niche markets like chef's knives, slip-joint folders, and tactical fixed blades retain enough interest to be powerful sub-markets. Price points and availability in primary and secondary markets lead to the demise of the front-runners. Popular market sectors inspire experienced and new makers to build that type of knife.

Two problems arise from this: 1) Makers will rapidly join a market sector, but collectors are slower to follow; and 2) Pricing is primarily based on what other makers are getting for their work and not, for example, the quality of a maker's knives, name recognition, status among the competition, etc.

In the spike tomahawk realm is this Csizmar Szilard model with a forged 5160 high-carbon steel head, a hickory haft, and a custom leather sheath. Szilard is a well-known maker in Romania. *(Csizmar Szilard photo)*

Higher prices from less qualified knifemakers encourage the well-known makers to raise their prices, and the cycle continues until the knives become unaffordable. Currently, this is what is happening today in the forged blade market. I saw this trend emerging in 2020, and I started emphasizing makers who offer value for the money with their work.

Overpriced knives led me to increase my research for custom knives with good value in the United States and worldwide. Social media was a great help in this area. As I researched, I found myself saving photos of knives I was interested in. When I returned to re-look at the pictures I had saved, I found many of these makers were from Eastern Europe.

Much like in the United States, prices ranged from reasonable to what seemed extreme. I contacted well over a hundred makers asking questions about materials, construction techniques, pricing, and sheaths, and requested several additional photos. While there are other makers I plan to contact soon, the following are the seven makers I have already started working with.

Meet the Makers

Maksim Tjulpin has been making knives for 11 years in his home country of Latvia. His interest comes from the diversity of knives that can be made as well as the array of materials. Maksim builds knives utilizing both the stock-removal and forging methods of blade making. He favors forged blades as each has its own unique character.

He primarily uses stabilized wood for his handles, often combined with mammoth ivory spacers. I have found his craftsmanship to be impeccable. The knives feature excellent fit and finish as well as ideal balance and handle ergonomics.

Petr Dohnal and his son, Peter, have been making knives for 21 years in their native country of the Czech Republic. Working as a computer graphic designer, Petr realized he wanted to build something with his hands. So, he chose to make custom knives. As with many makers, his favorite part is forging the blades, usually damascus. In addition to making his own steel, he uses Elmax, Vanadis 8, and M390, as well as other alloys. He understands that the knife's intended purpose will often determine the most suitable steel. His handle materials of choice are stabilized wood and antler. I find Petr's knives a joy to hold in my hand, being sleek, well-made, and exhibiting superior balance and handle ergonomics.

Michal Komorovsky started making knives, in 2011, in his home country, Slovakia, or officially, the Slovak Republic—doing so primarily because he wanted to try something different, and he never looked back. He favors Sleipner steel, which is a new-generation alloy like D-2, as well as M390. When time allows, he forges damascus for his knives, including a wide variety of fixed blades. Michal builds an array of knives, from hunting and tactical models to bowies and even an occasional art dagger.

Many of his tactical knives feature black DLC-coated blades, but he also offers sandblasted and bead-blasted steel, as well as satin- and mirror-polished finishes. Michal uses various handle materials, with desert ironwood being his favorite. I've taken a liking to his fighters that exhibit excellent fit and finish, have an outstanding balance, and feel great in the hand.

The Tactical Realm

Piotr Gosciniak has been fashioning custom knives in his home country of Poland since 2017. Having a keen interest in the military, Piotr decided to focus his talent on making tactical knives. He occasionally uses high-carbon steel such as 80CrV, but most of his knives are built using quality stainless steels such as Elmax or Sleipner.

Piotr prefers synthetic handle materials like Micarta, G-10, and carbon fiber. He also offers Cerakote coating for his knives. As a former infantry officer, I appreciate the crisp, clean lines of Piotr's knives. His designs are purpose-driven; these are tools meant to be used. The blade fullers, textured handle material, and thumb serrations add to each knife's capability.

Also from Poland, Jacek Hnatow has been building knives for eight years. He started as a collector, then decided he didn't want to buy knives anymore; he wanted to make them. As an avid outdoorsman, it should come as no surprise that Jacek's specialties are survival and bushcraft blades. He prefers working with Bohler N690 and Elmax, as well as high-carbon alloys and san mai steel. Jacek's handle material offerings include synthetics such as G-10 and Micarta, as well as stabilized wood at the customer's request. His knives, many of which can be huge, are well-balanced with great handle ergonomics. His bushcraft blades are a perfect size to carry in the field, and all of Jacek's knives are well thought out for

The sleek, stealthy, and sexy fighter by Michal Komorovsky exhibits a 7.75-inch, black DLC-coated Elmax blade, a black canvas Micarta handle, and a leather sheath. The balance of the knife makes it deceptively quick, and a fuller reduces the weight while increasing blade strength. *(Michal Komorovsky photo)*

Working with European Makers

Language: There are several languages throughout Europe. While it is true that many Europeans speak English, it is equally noteworthy that they do not read and write the universal language well. This is important to know as, more than likely, collectors will be contacting the makers via email or social media. When writing, I often rely on an online translator for help. Understand that such online translating programs could be better. I always let the maker know upfront I am using a translator.

When emailing or writing to makers, try not to use slang or acronyms, as these usually translate into something that might not have the intended meaning. Remember to be patient with this process, as both collector and maker must understand exactly what each is expecting.

Payments: The preferred method

Petr Dohnal forged a damascus camp knife, including the guard, adding a stabilized Karelian birch handle and fossil walrus ivory spacer. It comes with a custom leather sheath.
(Petr Dohnal photo)

the tasks at hand.

Romanian Csizmar Szilard has been a full-time knifemaker since 2007. When he was younger, he enjoyed video games and one of them allowed players to forge their weapons virtually. So, Csizmar decided to make that a reality. Forging is his favorite part of fashioning knives, hatchets, and axes. He prefers 5160 high-carbon steel for its simplicity and ease of forging. Handle materials are all-natural, with wood and antler being his favorites. Csizmar's work is clean and balanced, precisely what you would expect from a maker who builds tools that are meant to be used.

A native of Poland, Szymek Szlagor has been making knives since 2017. Building a knife for himself led to making them for friends and eventually becoming a full-time knifemaker. He enjoys forging and machining carbon steel and damascus. He gravitates toward 5160 high-carbon steel and combines K720 and 15N20 to make damascus. His handle material preferences are natural materials such as stabilized wood and antlers. For his everyday carry (EDC) knives, he prefers to use Micarta. Szymek feels making knives is a beautiful job that involves taking a piece of steel, giving it shape, and improving on it until the blade becomes a tool that will be used and passed down from generation to generation. Having handled his work, he has accomplished his goal.

for knife transactions is PayPal. As with most makers worldwide, many are not set up to take credit cards. Those who have traveled to Europe know there are additional fees for using U.S. bank credit cards. Although wire transfers can be made, it is best to check with your bank to find out what the fee for an international wire transfer will be.

Lastly, Western Union is an option that usually comes with an $8 fee. Some buyers might find the process of paying upfront and then having to wait up to a month difficult. However, I have been buying knives regularly from Eastern Europe for the last three years and have never had a package go missing.

Maksim Tjulpin's camp knife features a 7.1-inch san mai damascus blade, a stainless guard, a black G-10 spacer, and a mammoth tooth and desert ironwood handle. It comes with a custom leather sheath. *(Maksim Tjulpin photo)*

The 13-inch camp knife from Szymek Szlagor showcases a forged Bohler K720 blade with hamon (temper line), a stainless guard and sambar stag handle scales. *(Robertson's Custom Cutlery photo)*

Shipping: The maker will generally ship the knife through his or her country's postal service. Most countries work with the U.S. Postal Service, and once a package is accepted, you can track it coming from Europe. The delivery time frame will average between two and four weeks. While FedEx can be an option, the cost associated will generally eliminate this service from the ideal options.

Measurements: Europe uses the metric system. As foreign as the metric system is to you, the same is true for the imperial system the United States uses to makers in Europe. Fortunately, there are conversion programs on the internet. In conversing with European makers, please pay attention and differentiate between when they use centimeters (cm) or millimeters (mm), as 1 centimeter equals 10 millimeters, and when it comes to a knife, that could

be a huge difference.

Forged in Fire Influence

Most of the makers in this article offer forged blades as part of the repertoire. However, Piotr Gosciniak is the exception, as he specializes in stainless and some high-carbon steel tactical knives. The U.S. market will see a resurgence of this category of knives in 2023-'24. For now, forged blades are the most significant market sector in the United States, partly due to increased interest in forging knives due to the TV show "Forged in Fire." The interest created by this show was partly responsible for 38 makers earning their American Bladesmith Society (ABS) journeyman smith ratings at the 2022 BLADE Show.

Talking with several ABS master smiths, I was told they saw an increase in the number of makers

Jacek Hnatow offers the "Wicher" tactical
fixed blade in Bohler N690 stainless steel, a
black G-10 handle and a custom Kydex sheath.
Of full-tang construction, the contoured handle
provides excellent grip even when hands are wet.

(Robertson's Custom Cutlery photo)

taking their journeyman smith performance test before the 2023 BLADE Show as well. As a result, I anticipate the final numbers to show a record number of candidates testing for their journeyman smith stamps in 2023. With an increase in knife shows across the United States, hammer-ins, and the accessibility of in-person training and videos on social media, the number of forged blade makers will continue to increase over the next several years.

As these new makers enter the custom knife market, their pricing will be based more on what their peers charge for knives as opposed to a position in the market that their work has earned. In the short term, collectors will be the ones subsidizing too many who are bound to have short careers as custom knifemakers. Long term, the aftermarket will sort out the winners and losers. Therefore, it is incumbent on buyers to understand value pricing and that they should not buy a custom knife that will lose value.

Over the last 37 years, I have bought and sold knives on every continent except Antarctica. Today, it is easy to find exceptional makers in Eastern Europe and worldwide. I understand that ordering from makers outside the United States can be a leap of faith.

My hints regarding purchasing knives from Eastern Europe should help you with your concerns. The styles, materials, and craftsmanship of makers worldwide have never been better. This is why I suggest you give the makers in this article and others around the world consideration to become part of your collection. □

White River Knife & Tool's Jerry Fisk Sendero Classic Custom showcases a beautiful ironwood burl handle.

Hot Handle Materials
Include Hybrids

Natural and synthetic materials are equal parts fashionable and functional.

By Mike Haskew

They complement one another in an easy, seamless union—blade and handle. One without the other means the knife is incomplete, or it isn't a knife at all.

Along with the search for proper blade steel, appropriate handle material is the second critical element in the presentation, form, and function of the knife itself. Natural and synthetic handles play their roles. They bring utility and aesthetics to the package, and the maker's choice sets the tone. Availability, cost, and maker's preference fit into the equation when choosing the right handle material. And then, of course, the intended knife use weighs heavily.

In the end, it's the eye of the artist that drives the visual element, and the job to be done by the user that directs his or her choice. The handle makes the knife complete.

At Masecraft Supply Company, co-owner Chris

Hartman sees the supplier's role as the facilitator. Never interfering with the artist's concept, he views Masecraft as a provider of the palette. "We don't advise what to use," he reasons. "We are not big fans of, 'You know what you should do …' or telling a customer what to use, but more in supplying a wide variety of options to choose from. We are always willing to answer questions about our materials a customer may have, but it's just not a good idea to advise what is right for them. That's the maker's choice."

With that said, where is the market headed today? What does the landscape look like in terms of availability, trends, and timing?

"The majority seem to be sticking with composite laminates like G-10, canvas and linen Micarta, and Richlite," Hartman says. "Natural materials like bone and horn seem to be in a continuing decline.

This Northfield UN-X-LD knife from Great Eastern Cutlery (GEC), which registered the trademark and uses it on premium GEC pocketknives, features ALVS (acrylic laminated veneer shell) handle scales from Masecraft Supply Company. The dazzling shell veneer consists of real shell and high-impact acrylic laminated together within the sheet.

Exotic woods still do well, but availability and pricing have become issues over the last two years."

John Cammenga, vice president of operations at White River Knife & Tool, Inc., deals primarily in synthetic knife handle materials. He indicates that knifemakers who build hard-use models often lean toward durable synthetic handles and that the laminate trend holds up there as well, particularly with material available in a variety of colors.

"The majority of our handle materials are synthetic," Cammenga says, "and this is primarily due to stability and longevity. But many look great as well. Multi-color layers of fabric bonded with phenolic or polyester resin can have the look of wood, yet last much longer. Additionally, many of these are tackier when wet, giving the user additional hand purchase in tough weather or when processing game. Carbon fiber and G-10 are available in an ever-expanding array of colors and patterns and almost bulletproof when it comes to wear and tear."

Intended Knife Use

The choice of materials, Cammenga explains, comes directly down to the proposed use of the knife. For hunting, fishing, camping or bushcraft, White River almost always recommends synthetic handle material. However, John still gives a nod to personal preference. Some users simply must have a natural handle, and the aesthetic factor comes into play there.

"It's hard to beat the beauty of a highly figured burl!" he comments. "Some, such as desert ironwood burl, are not only beautiful but also extremely tough."

Tom Krein is an experienced

This Santa Fe Stoneworks El Rey model is handled in a spectacular turquoise/abalone/bronze hybrid gemstone and includes a mother-of-pearl button inlay.

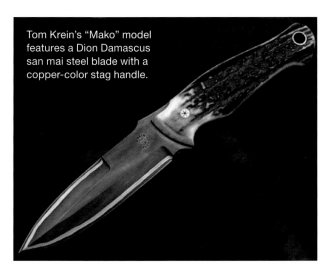

Tom Krein's "Mako" model features a Dion Damascus san mai steel blade with a copper-color stag handle.

The stylish White River Knife & Tool hunter parades a black burlap-Micarta grip.

custom knifemaker who worked for the great Bob Dozier and ran the custom shop for A.G. Russell Knives before embarking on his own venture during 30 years in the business. Making small utility and hunting knives primarily, he agrees that handle material choice relates to a few simple concepts.

"It comes down to the customer's needs, willingness to care for the knife, aesthetics, and budget," Krein relates. "Natural materials should hold up nicely with proper care assuming everything goes according to plan. Sometimes stuff happens—a knife falls into a sink of water, or it starts to rain while hunting, or your knife gets lost in the yard for a week. Synthetics hold up better when stuff goes south. For customers, I recommend getting what you like and learning how to take care of it. For knifemakers, I suggest picking the mind of another maker who uses the material you want so you can learn how to use it. Overall, we are a helpful bunch of people."

Traditional handle materials and their innovative, eye-popping counterparts coexist at Santa Fe Stoneworks, a provider of materials to the art knife market since 1978. Santa Fe not only affixes those materials to its own knives, but also provides the service for Spyderco and Kershaw while doing private label work as well.

President Bill Wirtel leads the family business, and the company's roster of natural handle materials includes the best of the best. "We work with factory knives and apply gemstones, exotic woods, shells like gold- and black-lip pearl, and fossils such as woolly mammoth tooth, tusk, bone, and petrified dinosaur bone," he remarks.

As for Santa Fe's synthetics, Fordite, a car paint overspray, Surfite surfboard overspray, and a cholla cactus-like material that is made in the shop have found favor with makers and buyers alike.

Materials Mash-Up

"We are looking for design and color, so we mix natural with manmade stone and epoxies," Wirtel explains. "Our fossils are all stabilized so they work great for a handle material. We see hybrid materials gaining popularity as they provide the best of both natural and composite materials. Fordite and Surfite have been selling well. Our synthetic cholla cactus line that we make here, stabilizing it with different colored epoxies, is becoming a big seller as well. We also have mammoth tusk fusion. This is stabilized fragments of mammoth ivory that are fused together under immense pressure. The result is a beautiful and hard composite that is densely packed with mammoth ivory."

Fordite is an interesting option that comes from a surprising source. Also known as Detroit agate or motor agate, the material consists of pre-1985 automobile paint that hardened sufficiently to be cut and polished. It formed from enamel paint slag, which built up over the years in layers on the tracks and skids where cars were hand spray-painted. The

Dozier Knives produced this fixed blade with a Richlite handle from Masecraft Supply Company composed of approximately 65% Forest Stewardship Council (FSC)®-certified recycled paper and 35% phenolic resin.

Knifemaker Tom Krein says there's a huge push to find and use vintage Micarta, such as on the handle of his pocket bowie model.

Fordite car paint handle material adds a fun flair to this series of Santa Fe Stoneworks 3-inch lock-back folders with damascus blades.

buildup hardened in ovens intended to cure the paint on car bodies. After so much of that buildup, the brightly colored and layered paint had to be removed. Its allure caught on with some autoworkers who brought pieces home with them. From there, the beautiful Fordite material, which can be cut and polished into a spectacular look, found its way onto knife handles.

The Masecraft perspective is somewhat dictated by availability. "Sambar stag is not coming back," Hartman stresses. "It has been banned by India for export since sometime around 2005, I believe, so that's almost 20 years now, and I see no chance of this ever changing. What's still available out there now is it. Game over!"

"Black-lip, gold, and white mother-of-pearl all are still available," he adds, "just not in larger size pieces as they were 20-50 years ago. They are overharvested and not as healthy as before. Demand for shell is down overall. It is not very tactical, and we seem to be in a tactical and bushcraft market for the last two decades. Shell tended to be more of a gentleman's pocketknife material, so it's not exactly the big trend right now."

"Many of the companies that used a lot of shell on knives are gone or simply don't have the people who know how to work with it anymore," Hartman adds. "Shell is still one of the most beautiful materials ever, so much so that it seems to be the hardest to reproduce in any type of synthetic alternative that even comes close to its natural beauty. We can come close, but there is still nothing like the real thing."

Krein sees a swing toward synthetics and higher-end natural materials as well. "Right now, there is a huge push to find and use vintage Micartas," he relates. "I've also seen G-10 usage go up a ton over the years. G-10 holds up to use extremely well, is relatively inexpensive, and machines and grinds easily. I've also noticed quite a few new businesses that specialize in exotic stabilized woods. Stag has always been a desired and quality knifemaking material, and with exceptional stag being much harder to find, it is even more desirable, particularly when done [harvested and finished] properly."

Watching the high-end polymer Ultem begin to trend as a new synthetic handle material has been interesting for Krein, and his affinity for giraffe bone has not waned. It's something he calls the "latest real pickup in natural materials."

"I often see new makers using very exotic materials," Krein concludes. "These materials are costly and often not used anywhere close to their potential.

White River Knife & Tool purchases synthetic material made in the USA, so supply chain issues have not been a problem. The one material the company imports, cork, has increased in price, but its supply has been uninterrupted. White River's Traditional Fillet knife incorporates a handle of imported cork for easy cleanup and a tight grip in slippery conditions.

I recommend that new makers learn to use simpler materials like Micarta to their full potential. This leaves funds available for other materials and equipment while allowing a new maker to develop their skills. Just because a knife has expensive materials doesn't make it better or more interesting to me. It's developing the skills to make simple materials look elegant that I appreciate."

Hybrid Handles

Hybrid handle material is on the rise, and Cammenga is pleased with the growing popularity of marbled synthetics. "Right now, there is strong demand," he notes. "This is true in both cloth/resin laminates and carbon-fiber/resin laminates. For those who want natural wood, bone or antler, acrylic 'stabilized' scales have been popular for quite some time. They provide the user with a natural material, which has been made tougher by introducing acrylic resin into the fibers. Currently the marbled look is in with almost all materials, but we have made several knife models using G-10 and rubber combinations, as well as others from polyester cloth and resins."

Masecraft is keeping a close eye on the development of new materials, but the course is charted by ingenuity rather than discovery. "As far as new natural materials, that's going to be extremely rare," Hartman observes. "The earth is not really producing anything new, so unless we have not discovered it yet, the odds are low. More likely, some natural materials will disappear and become endangered, banned, or extinct. Human history tells us the availability of natural material will decrease while prices increase. You will see more hybrids of natural and synthetic combinations, and all kinds of new synthetics will continue to be introduced."

Supply often dictates how well demand is satisfied, and the inherent scarcity of some handle materials has been exacerbated by supply chain concerns in areas. Even as the COVID-19 pandemic has eased, the resilience of the supply chain remains an open question. Some suppliers and makers have faced shortages of stock items, while others have adapted, moved on to other, more readily available options, or simply been patient.

"I have been sourcing materials for over 44 years, and most of our suppliers know us and what we want," Wirtel relates. "Obviously, we've had supply chain issues, but we have been able to work around them. We make our product to order, so we range in delivery time from a few weeks to a few months."

Krein is positive regarding availability, saying, "There have been slight wait times for some synthetics, particularly Micarta, during the pandemic, but it seems like everything is back on track here. There has and will continue to be more demand for quality stag than availability. I've seen a bit less of

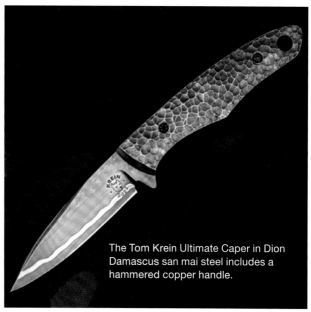

The Tom Krein Ultimate Caper in Dion Damascus san mai steel includes a hammered copper handle.

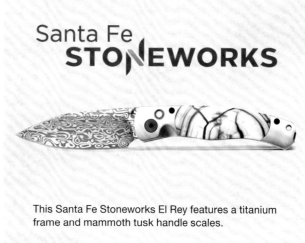

This Santa Fe Stoneworks El Rey features a titanium frame and mammoth tusk handle scales.

quality exotic stabilized woods like exhibition-grade ironwood and Koa."

While the supply chain phenomenon has been universal, Hartman is pragmatic. Going with the flow makes the Masecraft operation run as smoothly as possible. "There are supply chain issues with everything globally," he observes. "I can't think of anything on the planet that hasn't been affected in some way, shape or form and that doesn't have a price increase or isn't in short supply, and it's all things, countries, and markets."

"If you don't have the chip, you can't produce the car," Hartman says. "If you don't have OD Green dye, you can't make OD Green G-10. If one key part is missing due to supply chain issues, the product simply cannot be made, and that is affecting all things."

Staying domestic has been a problem solver for White River Knife & Tool, according to Cammenga. "Because White River purchases synthetic material made within the U.S., our supply chain has not been a problem. The one material we do import, cork, has increased in price, but our supply has been uninterrupted."

Considering the handle-blade combination that makes the knife come together for the spectrum of customers and users, today's material options appear more diverse than ever. Although some shortages in natural materials may never be plentiful again, fusions of natural and synthetic options open the door to creativity. And the imagination is always fertile ground for innovation. □

Rescue Knives
Save Lives

Blades are purpose-built with materials and features meant to aid people in dire need.

By Dexter Ewing
Photos by Marty Stanfield, Marty Stanfield Photography

escue knives are an integral part of first responders' most important gear. They serve as multi-purpose cutting tools like other knives and are heavily relied upon during various rescue operations. Let's look at the latest rescue knives available on the market.

Emerson Knives took its existing SARK (Search and Rescue Knife) folder, adapting it to the U.S. Navy's specifications, and thus the NSAR (Navy Search and Rescue) was born. The 3.5-inch 154CM hawkbill-style blade features a blunt tip and a recessed cutting hook ground into the spine. Other features include an integral thumb rest and Emerson's signature Wave remote opener designed to catch on the hem of a pants pocket and pull the folding blade open as the knife is withdrawn.

The ergonomic G-10 handle showcases an integral front hand guard, palm swell in the middle, and grooves at the thumb rest and rear positions to provide a non-slip grip in any condition. At a little over 8 inches long, the NSAR is a knife that can handle many emergency cutting tasks. A steel pocket clip secures the folder tip-up in the pocket, a configuration that works well with the Wave remote opener. An optional ambidextrous thumb disk deploys the blade more traditionally.

One of the things I like is the hawkbill blade with a reverse curve that gathers material as it cuts. Customers have a choice of a plain or partially serrated blade, the latter ideal for cutting through tough, fibrous materials. The blunt tip makes it easy to work around accident victims without fear of further injury.

In my tests, the recessed hook worked well, cutting anything that would gather inside its curved diameter. The flat-ground blade is sharpened on one side only like a chisel grind, yielding a keen and easy-to-hone edge. At the local scrapyard where I conducted real-life tests, the NSAR ripped through materials with ease, including seatbelts. It is a major league rescue tool in terms of design, construction, and function. The manufacturer's suggested retail price (MSRP) for the Emerson NSAR is $299.95.

Lifesaving rescue knives include, from top to bottom, the Emerson Knives NSAR, Spyderco Byrd Cara Cara Rescue 2, Benchmade Auto Triage, Hogue Trauma First Response Tool, and the Leatherman Raptor Rescue Shears.

The heavy-duty Benchmade Auto Triage integrates features that allow it to double as a rescue folder and a versatile work knife. The partially serrated, modified clip-point blade can handle any utility cutting chore.

Anchoring the budget end of the spectrum is the Byrd Cara Cara Rescue 2. A value brand belonging to Spyderco, Byrd knives incorporate the same innovation and style of construction as more expensive Spyderco models, but with different materials that yield amazing value. Most folding rescue knives are on the high end of the price spectrum, placing them out of reach financially to many front-line blue-collar workers.

Measuring 3.9 inches long, the Cara Cara Rescue 2 blade is ground from 8Cr13MoV stainless steel and sports a fully serrated edge that munches through fibrous materials. The comet-shaped hole in the blade permits ease of one-handed opening and provides a more secure thumb purchase than a standard round hole, especially when wearing gloves.

Blunt Point Prevents Punctures

The blunt point of the sheepsfoot blade prevents accidental punctures during use. The fiberglass-reinforced nylon (FRN) handle promotes a comfortable, non-slip grip thanks to the unique bi-directional texturing along with grooving, or jimping, on the handle spine. The handle feels solid and showcases dual nested steel liners and screw-together construction. A four-way pocket clip allows the user to select

from left- or right-handed, tip-up or tip-down carry. Once open, the blade locks into place solidly. The mid-handle placement of the lock release itself makes it possible to unlock the blade and close it using one hand.

I noticed the handle's lack of significant chamfering and contouring. Less machining is necessary with a moldable FRN handle, translating into a lower price point. Yes, the Byrd Cara Cara Rescue 2 can feel a bit blocky in hand, but the straightforward design results in a secure grip and a knife that is easy to manipulate when wearing thick gloves typical to a first responder.

Spyderco engineers some of the finest fully serrated folding knives on the market, with the Byrd Cara Cara Rescue 2 being one of them. The blade easily eats through the toughest materials—cardboard, seatbelts, and thick tie-down straps being no match. The comfortable, ergonomic handle rests securely in the palm to instill user confidence. Comfortable to carry in a pants pocket or inner waistband, the thin profile doesn't add bulk, yet feels good in the grip.

The 8Cr13MoV steel is a Chinese equivalent to Japanese AUS-8, a good mid-range alloy that balances edge holding with ease of maintenance and cost. To those looking for a quality rescue knife on a

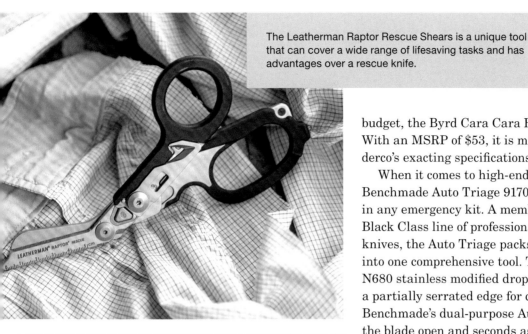

The Leatherman Raptor Rescue Shears is a unique tool that can cover a wide range of lifesaving tasks and has advantages over a rescue knife.

The cutting hook of the Benchmade Auto Triage is the only such tool on the market deployed automatically. An effective cutter, the hook deploys instantaneously in high-stress rescue operations.

budget, the Byrd Cara Cara Rescue 2 is the answer. With an MSRP of $53, it is made in China to Spyderco's exacting specifications.

When it comes to high-end rescue knives, the Benchmade Auto Triage 9170SBK is a serious piece in any emergency kit. A member of Benchmade's Black Class line of professional rescue and tactical knives, the Auto Triage packs a bunch of innovations into one comprehensive tool. The 3.5-inch Bohler N680 stainless modified drop-point blade sports a partially serrated edge for cutting versatility. Benchmade's dual-purpose Auto Axis Lock secures the blade open and seconds as a blade release for the auto-opening folder. Pulling back on the lock release opens the blade automatically.

The Auto Triage rests securely in the hand and is easy to operate and completely ambidextrous. An ergonomic handle is constructed of T6-6061 aluminum with a Type III hard-coat black anodized finish. Black G-10 handle inlays provide additional hand purchase, and the grip also features a safety cutting hook for seatbelts and clothing. Pulling back on the lock release button close to the rear of the handle activates the cutting hook that is otherwise tucked away until needed. This is the only cutting hook on the market that is automatically deployed.

At first blush, I thought the automatic cutting hook might be overkill, but in considering the thick gloves first responders wear, combined with the stress and adrenaline rush of being in the moment, having an auto-deploying hook makes total sense. The pull-down release works well with gloved hands as opposed to fumbling around while attempting to use a manual rescue hook. A deep-carry pocket clip allows tip-up right-hand carry and a carbide glass breaker at the end of the handle shatters car and other windows with ease.

Overbuilt Handle

Right off the bat, from the build of the handle, users can see the Auto Triage is a stout knife easily manipulated wearing gloves. While it might feel blocky in hand, when gripping the handle with gloves, one becomes aware of its presence and the knife feels secure. Because there is a secondary cutting hook

Blade serrations on the Hogue Trauma First Response Tool (top) aggressively eat through fibrous materials, while the Leatherman Raptor Rescue Shears (bottom) quickly cuts through thick media like nylon webbing and jeans.

to manage seatbelts and clothing, the main blade is designed with a sharpened tip. The true rescue tool that it is, Benchmade's Auto Triage is every bit as much a working folder for general cutting tasks.

Partial edge serrations on the modified drop-point blade easily power through stubborn materials. The flat grind of the blade is another aspect of its exceptional cutting performance, with a thin but strong edge that sails through cutting media with little effort. The Auto Axis Lock release is intuitive and truly ambidextrous, allowing for quick and easy blade release with either hand. It is especially crucial in emergencies for professionals who use whatever hand is available to deploy the blade or cutting hook.

The vanadium and nitrogen inherent to the N680 steel help boost its anti-corrosion properties. The cutting hook works quickly, gathering material as it cuts and slices through seatbelts as easily as pulling a zipper. The keen hook bites into webbing and clothing with little effort and a sliding switch safety on the main blade prevents the Auto Axis Lock from inadvertently deploying the blade. Located on the handle spine just behind the lock release buttons, the sliding safety switch is easily accessed.

Overall, the Benchmade Auto Triage 9170SBK is a professional, high-quality tool that feels great and secure in the hand and doubles as a general-use folding knife, which further makes it that much

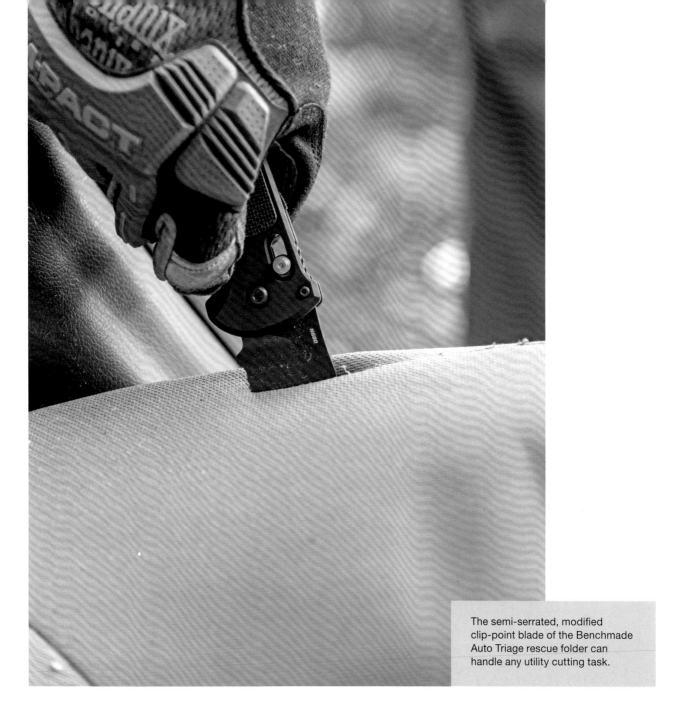

The semi-serrated, modified clip-point blade of the Benchmade Auto Triage rescue folder can handle any utility cutting task.

more attractive. The Auto Triage isn't a single-purpose tool like other rescue knives. With an MSRP of $350, the Benchmade Auto Triage is a high-end rescue tool.

Leatherman Tool Group, the company that pioneered pliers-based multi-tools, takes a different approach to a rescue tool in the form of its Raptor Rescue Shears. Modeled after high-leverage emergency medical technician (EMT) trauma shears, the Raptor Rescue incorporates several features that make it a unique rescue tool.

The Raptor Rescue features several of the most used implements for removing clothing from rescue victims. For starters, the blades of the main shears are each over 1/8-inch thick, and sport super sharp cutting edges. This tool quickly cuts through thick material like nylon webbing and jeans. The full-size handle's finger loops accommodate gloved hands and folding the Raptor Rescue allows easy access and employment of the tools and other built-in functions.

Such tools and functions include a carbide glass breaker for shattering side windows of vehicles, a fold-out cutting hook for seatbelts and other fibrous materials, and an oxygen bottle wrench. There's even a built-in wire cutter behind the pivot of the shears, taking advantage of leverage at that location. The Leatherman Raptor Rescue folds into a

The Hogue Trauma First Response Tool has a rescue hook that folds out manually from the rear of the handle to provide quick cutting of seatbelts and clothing.

compact, easy-to-carry package. The handle halves fold onto themselves, and there's an ingenious lock on each handle that prevents the tool grips from folding up while in use.

The heavy-duty plastic holster accompanying the Raptor is designed to keep the tool close at hand until it is needed and does so in one of two positions. First, when the tool is folded, the Raptor slides into the holster and is secured by a pocket clip fastened over the lip of the sheath. A second carry option is with the handles fully open. The blade inserts through a specially shaped hole in the bottom of the sheath, and the shears are locked into place inside the holster for carrying the Raptor in the open position and secured with a locking tab. This method is the most ideal, as one doesn't have to fiddle with opening the handles. Just grab the shears and go.

Speaking of being on the go, the MSRP of the Leatherman Raptor is $89.95 in case you want to take one home with you.

Tactical and Rescue Knives

Hogue Knives is a major player in the tactical and rescue knife market. The company designed its Trauma First Response Tool from the ground up as a full-service rescue knife that has all the tools any first responder could need on a call. The Trauma is offered in a choice of a sheepsfoot blade or an opposing-bevel blunt-tip configuration. For this article, Hogue sent me the opposing-bevel blade with a partially serrated edge and an orange G-10 handle.

The Bohler N680 blade is corrosion resistant with additional nitrogen added to the alloy mix. The opposing-bevel grind of the 3.4-inch blade gives it additional strength in the cross-section, and a blunt tip helps greatly reduce injury to accident victims while cutting seatbelts and clothing. Dual thumb studs permit it to be easily opened with either hand and the blade is secured open by Hogue's ABLE Lock, a truly ambidextrous crossbar design that is strong and safe.

The highly visible, ergonomic orange G-10 handle

integrates dual stainless liners for strength, and a large finger groove helps index the user's grip. The thumb rest area of the handle spine has traction notches for a non-slip grip. The handle also incorporates a few important tools that are handy for rescue personnel. First, there is a fold-out cutting hook for performing pull-cuts through seatbelt webbing and clothing as easily as pulling a zipper. A single thumb stud deploys the cutting hook easily, and though a detent secures the hook in the open position, unlike the Benchmade Auto Triage, it doesn't fully lock open.

There's also an oxygen bottle wrench incorporated into the left side of the handle, and the final tool on board is a carbide glass breaker in the handle spacer. The glass breaker easily shatters vehicle side windows. Hogue offers two convenient carry options for the Trauma—a deep-carry, tip-up pocket clip and a sturdy ballistic nylon belt sheath.

The Trauma's cutting performance is top-notch, with the partially serrated blade easily zipping through tough materials. The plain edge portion of the blade is sharpened on one side only, making it easier to maintain. Being a rescue tool, not a working utility knife, edge dings are not a primary concern. The straight-line edge makes the blade perform like a sheepsfoot model, and the serrations aggressively eat through fibrous materials. The cutting hook works nearly as well as the Benchmade Auto Triage, but as noted, does not lock open. This could be a slight inconvenience so long as the user does not lift it accidentally when employing the hook. Any cutting media is easily severed inside the hook. While using the knife with gloved hands is a cinch, accessing the hook can be a bit deliberate, as one needs to open it with the thumb.

I particularly like the look of an orange handle with a black blade. While orange makes the knife stand out, the Trauma is also available in a black G-10 handle. The MSRP for the Hogue Trauma tested here is $199.99. □

Leatherman's Raptor Rescue Shears is an effective emergency tool built around a full-size pair of EMT shears. The heavy-duty shears can take on tough tasks like cutting up this thick hose. The bottom blade is serrated, which helps to hold the cutting medium.

Equipped with a carbide glass breaker in the butt of the handle, the Benchmade Auto Triage can effectively shatter automotive side windows for quick access and vehicular extractions.

Basic Layout and Measuring Tools for Knifemakers

Technology and knowhow make it possible to achieve fine knife "fit and finish."

By Tim Zowada

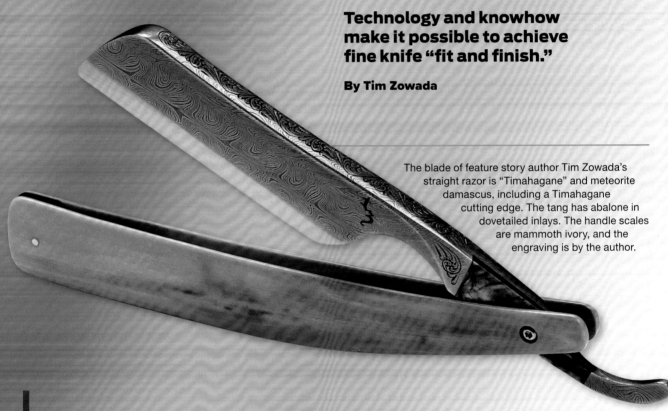

The blade of feature story author Tim Zowada's straight razor is "Timahagane" and meteorite damascus, including a Timahagane cutting edge. The tang has abalone in dovetailed inlays. The handle scales are mammoth ivory, and the engraving is by the author.

In conversations about custom knives, there is a lot of discussion regarding "fit and finish." The topic revolves around how well the various parts of a knife fit together. It also includes such things as blade symmetry, overall knife symmetry, blade and handle finish, design aesthetic, and overall craftsmanship.

When making a well-crafted knife, paramount to making things fit well is having the ability to accurately measure, locate, and layout features. As with most things, there are many ways to get the job done. The following will provide a basis for those just entering the knifemaking field or others looking to increase the precision and accuracy of their work.

Standard Tools

Surface Plate - How is it possible to determine that a part is flat and straight if there isn't anything to compare it to? In ancient times, still water was used as a flat and straight reference. While water would work, it is easy to imagine the potential problems. These days, the standard flat reference is a surface plate.

A surface plate is simply a flat, horizontal surface, usually 12"x12" or larger. A surface plate is certified to a given level of flatness by the manufacturer and often by repeat inspections. Such plates are the standard reference datum for many measurements. In knifemaking, they are commonly used to measure

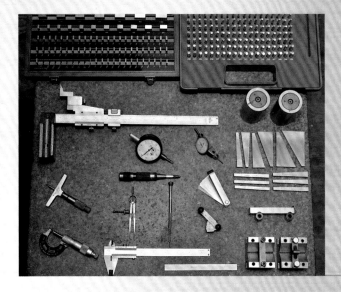

Here is a view of all the tools mentioned in the article, in the order presented. Starting at the top left corner, work clockwise around the surface plate, ending in the center.

the flatness and thickness of blades and other parts. They are also employed during the measurement of such parameters as height, squareness, concentricity, and comparative dimensions. Surface plates are also commonly used as reference planes during precision layout work of all sorts of features.

Before World War II, surface plates were often made of cast iron. Cast iron plates are still often available for sale online through places like eBay. The modern problem with a cast iron plate is finding someone who can properly certify its flatness and correct any problems that arise. For the most part, the world has moved on to granite surface plates.

Granite surface plates are available from most tool supply houses. The quality level starts with Chinese imports and continues up through U.S.-made laboratory quality. The grading system is a combination of size, flatness, and repeatability. The table below explains things better than I can.

The table reflects a flatness standard over the entire surface. There is also the local or "repeat reading" flatness over any 6-inch distance. Typically, it is far better than 50% of the overall flatness rating.

For perspective, the largest tolerance in the table is 400 microinches. That is equivalent to one-tenth

the thickness of a standard piece of typing paper! That's for the 24"x36" grade B plate. Amazing!

For the majority of knifemaking, an A or B-grade plate is more than sufficient. The AA plates are for those who have fallen down the rabbit hole of metrology—the science of measuring stuff. In knifemaking, measuring tolerances smaller than .0002 inch is usually not cost or time efficient. But it sure is fascinating! A world is entered where temperature and cleanliness play a huge role, and time often has no meaning.

Gage Blocks - While the surface plate is the standard for flatness, gage blocks are the standard for thickness. Gage blocks are simply small, rectangular blocks of steel, chromium carbide or ceramic. During manufacture, they are lapped flat to exacting tolerances. Once again, there are different grades, depending on the accuracy tolerance. The most precise blocks are accurate to within a couple millionths (0.000002) of an inch!

Just like surface plates, the most accurate gage blocks are not required for knifemaking. To be honest, most of the tools in this article are not required for knifemaking, but they make it much easier to achieve high precision and accuracy in the finished knife.

Surface Dimensions (Inches)		Surface Tolerance (Microinches)		
Width	Length	Grade AA	Grade A	Grade B
12	12	50	100	200
12	18	50	100	200
18	18	50	100	200
18	24	100	200	400
24	36	100	200	400

A precision test indicator is used to check the flatness of a folder blade.

The carbide scribe attachment on a height gage is used to scribe a centerline.

A 0.142" gage block is used to confirm the slot size in this hidden-tang guard.

Gage blocks have the unique ability to stick, or "wring," together. There are a lot of explanations for how this works. Suffice it to say, the blocks are not magnetic, yet they stay together. Placing one or more blocks on top of another allows the worker to create a stack in 0.0001" increments starting at 0.1000" and continuing up well over 10". For values thinner than 0.100", individual blocks can be purchased. The standard English 81-piece set includes blocks from 0.100" thick to 4". Metric sizes are also available.

One of the most common and useful functions of gage blocks is the regular calibration of micrometers, calipers, and other measuring tools. They are also extremely useful for gaging slots, and setting up sine plates, height gages, scribes, test indicators, and many other things.

Plug or Pin Gages - Plug and pin gages are precision-ground cylindrical bars, usually about 2" long. They are commonly used to measure the inside diameters of holes. Pin gages come in what are called "plus" or "minus" sets. That means they are ground to a tolerance that is usually 0.0002" larger or smaller than the stated size.

While these also come in sets, knifemakers usually only need a few common sizes. Buying 1/16", 3/32", 1/8", 3/16", and 1/4" pins is a good place to start without breaking the bank. Extra pins 0.001" and 0.0002" over and under these nominal dimensions are handy to have.

Gage pins are great for confirming a drilled or reamed hole is within specifications. In conjunction with a surface plate, test indicator, and height gage, gage pins can be used to measure hole locations accurately.

Square - Squares come in many shapes and sizes. This type of square is not the one normally used for layout. It is a master reference for a right angle. They are usually made of either steel or granite and are often cylindrical in shape. Used in conjunction with a surface plate, squares are regularly employed for setting up other measuring tools. Used directly with the aid of a bright light, they can be employed to quickly check if a square part is truly 90°.

Angle Blocks - Like gage blocks, but for angles, by stacking angle blocks, angles from 1/4° to over 100° can be created in 1/4° increments for measurement or set-up purposes.

Sine Bar – A sine bar is used in conjunction with gage blocks for setting up and measuring angles. A little trigonometry is required. Once the desired angle is known, look up the sine of the angle. Then multiply that number by the distance between the rollers on the sine bar. The result will be the height of the gage blocks to be put under one end of the sine bar.

As an example, for a 30° angle: Sin 30° = 0.5. The distance between the rollers on my little sine bar is 2.5", so: 0.5 x 2.5" = 1.25". Putting a 1.25" stack of

A sine bar is set up for a 30° angle. 1.000" and 0.250" gage blocks were used to raise the right end. The 30° angle block in the back is shown to confirm the setup. Below is the certification tag from this surface plate. The 20" x 30" granite plate is flat overall to 0.000044". Any measurements over 6 inches are repeatable to 0.000020".

Measuring the ricasso thickness with a micrometer is the first step in making a fine-fitting guard.

gage blocks under one of the rollers will raise the sine bar to a 30° angle.

V-Blocks - For holding cylindrical parts, such as pins, V-Blocks are employed in measuring, inspection, set-up, and machining work.

Measuring Tools

Pocket Scale – A 6" pocket scale is one of the most useful measuring tools in the shop. Carried in a shirt pocket or apron, it is handy for several common measurements. Since many parts on a knife don't require a tolerance of less than 0.100", a pocket scale is perfect. In the case of "Do as I say, not as I do," the 6" end might come in handy for light scraping or even stirring coffee.

Calipers – This is probably the most often used measuring tool in a knife shop. Calipers are useful for inside, outside, depth, and step measurements. They are also handy for setting other tools such as dividers and adjustable parallels.

Calipers come in several variations and sizes. The most important consideration is the method of reading the measurement. Calipers are commonly offered with either vernier scales, a mechanical dial, or digital/electric readout. Each has advantages. Vernier calipers are pretty much impervious to dust, dirt, oil, cutting fluids, etc. But the vernier scale requires a higher skill level to read and is slower in use than other types.

Mechanical dial reading calipers are likely the most common style in knife shops. They are fantastic for comparative measurements where the actual number isn't as important as comparing side "A" to side "B." Sadly, dial calipers are susceptible to dirt and other crud getting in the gearing. Care must be taken to keep them clean. Digital calipers range from horrible to fantastic. It all depends on the manufacturer and model. In general, you get what you pay for. With digital calipers, it is a good idea to keep a spare battery on hand.

Micrometer – Many knifemakers get by for years without a micrometer. But, once they learn to use one, a whole new world opens to them. With average user skill, measurements of ± 0.001" are easy. That range of 0.002" equates to half the thickness of a piece of standard typing paper. With experience and care, more precise measurements can easily be made. Micrometers are available in vernier, mechanical digital, and electric digital reading models.

Depth Micrometer – For reading the depth of features, and steps, depth micrometers are available in various reading option models.

Height Gage – A height gage is used in conjunction with a surface plate. Think of it as sort of a vertical caliper. The advantage is being able to attach scribes and other indicators to a height gage's movable jaw. When the movable jaw is zeroed on the surface plate, the height gage becomes a direct reading tool.

Height gages are also available with vernier, dial, mechanical digital, and electric digital reading options.

Standard Dial Indicator – Standard indicators are used for many measurements in the knife shop. In conjunction with a surface plate and height gage, they are used for measuring the height or thickness of objects. When attached to various machine tools, it becomes simple to measure the movement of a machine table or spindle. Standard indicators come in several travel ranges and reading options.

Measuring the ricasso thickness with a micrometer is the first step in making a fine-fitting guard.

A test indicator makes it a simple job to center the mill spindle directly above a hole center.

Test Indicator – A test indicator is used similarly to the standard indicator. The difference lies in that the test indicator's stylus is used horizontally to the surface being measured. This allows for things like getting inside holes and unusual surfaces.

It is simple to use a test indicator to determine the location of a hole center. On a milling machine, attach the test indicator to the machine spindle. Then, put the indicator's stylus inside the hole, touching the inside surface of one of the walls. Rotate the machine's spindle by hand while adjusting the location of the milling machine tables. Once the test indicator reads the same when rotated around the entire circumference of the hole, the machine spindle is directly over the center of the hole.

Feeler Gauges – When used in conjunction with a surface plate, feeler gauges are a quick way to measure the amount of warp in a part.

Thread Pitch Gauge – Used for determining the thread pitch of a nut or bolt, with the addition of a diameter measurement from a micrometer or caliper, it is easy to know exactly what size thread you are dealing with using a thread pitch gauge.

Marking Tools

Scribe – A scribe is a pencil-shaped tool with a hardened steel or carbide point used for marking references on a part for further machining or grinding.

Dividers – Dividers are used in much the same way as a scribe. The adjustable point distance allows for following edges and contours, as well as geometric uses of marking circles and arcs. Having good dividers handy also helps remove the temptation to use calipers as dividers.

Center Punch – A center punch is a hardened steel punch for marking future hole locations. The most basic type is struck with a hammer. Other versions are automatic, or spring-loaded.

As with many things, it is possible to fall completely down the rabbit hole of precision measurement. It is important to remember that it's easy to reach a point of diminishing returns. Waiting hours for temperatures to equalize, constant cleaning, and taking extreme care while handling parts, all to measure to .000005", will not necessarily produce a better knife.

Hours can be sucked away searching the internet for morsels of information. A lot of money and time can be wasted. Still, for those of us whose brains are wired a little differently, the search can be wonderful. But the knives won't get made as quickly, and the profit margin may suffer.

On the other hand, taking precision measurement to practical limits can and will help one produce better work. Developing the ability and mindset required to measure to something like 0.000050" will make the 0.0002" needed for precision folder work seem easy.

For those interested in taking things further, here are a few more tools that are useful in the knife shop.

Optical Comparator – An optical comparator is like a big overhead projector. It projects the profile and/or the surface of parts onto a glass screen where measurements can be made. A huge advantage is the part does not have to be touched to be measured. This is important with small and delicate parts.

With the right tooling, an optical comparator is fantastic for taking measurements in the middle of a process. The part can then be returned to the machine for final cutting.

Gage Amplifier – A gage amplifier is much like a test indicator, but it is electric with a separate readout. Careful use allows for measurements down to as small as 0.000002". Used gage amplifier units can be picked up on eBay for surprisingly little money.

Optical Flat and Monochromatic Light – An optical flat is a precision-lapped piece of glass. When laid on the surface to be inspected, while illuminated by a monochromatic light, interference bands appear. They look like stripes running across the part. These bands allow the flatness of the surface to be evaluated to within millionths of an inch.

Metrology is an amazing field. Taking the time to make careful measurements and perform precise setup work will greatly increase the fit, finish, and functionality of a knife. It doesn't take a lot to get started. A simple 6" scale, caliper, dividers, and scribe are a great place to begin. Once skill and interest increase, higher-quality tools can be acquired.

The ability to measure precisely allows the

This Tim Zowada lock-back folder features a damascus blade, wrought iron handle scales, and engraving by the author.

craftsperson to quantify and better understand the relationship of how things fit and work together. This often leads to a quest for even more precision and tighter tolerances. Although perfection is truly unobtainable and the search never ends, striving to make things as good as possible is what distinguishes the very best from all the rest. □

References

Excellent information can be found from a few sources on Instagram and YouTube. Be sure to scroll through all the videos. Although these are machining sites, there is a lot of stuff that applies to knifemaking.

Laney Machine Tech – From the instructor at Laney College in Oakland, CA
https://www.instagram.com/laneymachinetech/

OX Tools – Tom Lipton
https://www.youtube.com/@oxtoolco/videos
https://www.instagram.com/oxtools/

Robin Renzetti
https://www.youtube.com/user/ROBRENZ/videos
https://www.instagram.com/robinrenzetti/

Suburban Tool
https://www.youtube.com/@SuburbanToolInc/videos

"Handbook of Dimensional Measurement – Second Edition" by Francis T. Farago
This is an excellent book covering the field of metrology. Although it is from 1982, the book is still applicable to the home shop knifemaker. An added benefit is, due to its age, it can usually be picked up on Abebooks.com for under $10. It also looks like there are 1994 and 2013 updates available for more money.
https://www.abebooks.com/servlet/SearchResults?kn=Handbook%20of%20Dimensional%20Measurement%20%20Farago&sts=t&cm_sp=SearchF-_-topnav-_-Results

Collecting Randall Knives:
A Great Joy of His Life

The author has amassed an impressive collection of Special Edition Randalls.

By Evan F. Nappen, attorney at law

My love of knives began as a young boy when my father gave me a Swiss Army Knife that he purchased on his Bermuda honeymoon, in 1959. While trick-or-treating on Halloween, I showed my Swiss Army Knife to a friend. He showed me his long, thin-bladed, folding melon knife. I found a knife like his for $2 at a local flea market. After that, I became an unofficial collector of inexpensive flea market knives and built up quite a collection.

When I was 15 years old, my dad said, "Evan, look at this Randall Made Knives catalog. These knives are great. You should save your money and get one of these." The price of a Randall Model 1 back in 1976 was $70, a princely sum for me. However, I took my father's advice and saved enough money to buy a Model 1 "All-Purpose Fighting Knife." I anxiously waited six months to get it (now the wait time is approximately five years). When it arrived, I fell in love with its amazing craftsmanship, and the Model 1 instantly became my favorite knife.

Limited to 300 serial-numbered pieces, the Randall 50th Anniversary Knife is from the Evan Nappen collection.

In 1977, while on a 375-mile high-school bicycle trip through Florida, I was biking down the Orange Blossom Trail when I saw the famous Randall Made Knives sign. I decided to pay a visit to the Randall shop, and I had the honor as a teenager to meet Bo Randall, who personally gave me a tour of his business and the knife museum. Since then, collecting Randall knives has been a great joy in my life.

In 1988, Randall celebrated a half-century in business by issuing the 50th Anniversary Model limited to 300 serial-numbered pieces. The knife features a beautiful crown stag handle, weighs 16

Kittery Trading Post released three limited-production dealer special knives from 1995 to 1996. This set of three with matching serial numbers is from the collection of Evan Nappen.

ounces, and comes with a Model A leather sheath. At an overall length of 12.5 inches, the 7.5-inch blade is etched with two lines that include Bo Randall's signature over "1938-1988." The price was $375 new, and the 50th Anniversary Model is easily valued at 10 times that today. It is a special knife, indeed, that pays respect to the influence of William Scagel on Bo Randall's knifemaking career.

The Randall 75th Anniversary knife is a special Model 17 Astro with a "Vintage American Flag" stabilized, composite Micarta handle. It sports a 5.75-inch stainless blade, stretches 10 3/16 inches overall and weighs 10.6 ounces. The grip is fastened with removable stainless bolts, and as per the original design, there is a slot in the heavy tang that creates a hollow handle for storing survival items. It includes a Model C riveted sheath with a 75th Anniversary logo. In a limited edition of 200, the blade is etched with a serial number and the anniversary logo.

The knife was originally designed for the seven Mercury astronauts who each carried one on America's first manned space flights. Astronaut Gordon Cooper did the final design, and two of the knives are on display at the Smithsonian Institution. The Astro flew on several space missions. In 1961, Gus Grissom carried one into space on the Liberty Bell 7, which malfunctioned when it touched down in the ocean and sank approximately 16,000 feet. Astronaut Grissom escaped, but his Randall went down with the ship. Thirty-eight years later, the knife was recovered from the sea. That Randall Astro was approximately 120 miles above the earth and 16,000 feet beneath the ocean's surface, quite an achievement for a knife! Originally priced at $1,200, customers had to enter a drawing held on September 30, 2021, and win a chance to purchase the 75th Anniversary Model. Though the company's 75th anniversary was in 2013, it took Randall Made Knives eight years in the making

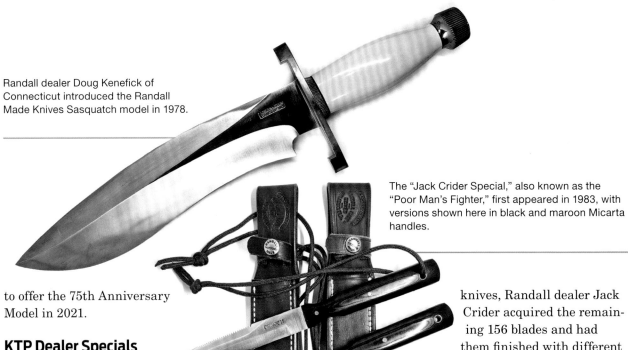

Randall dealer Doug Kenefick of Connecticut introduced the Randall Made Knives Sasquatch model in 1978.

The "Jack Crider Special," also known as the "Poor Man's Fighter," first appeared in 1983, with versions shown here in black and maroon Micarta handles.

to offer the 75th Anniversary Model in 2021.

KTP Dealer Specials

Kittery Trading Post (KTP), located in Kittery, Maine, has been a Randall dealer since 1979. KTP is my favorite sporting goods store, carrying a large variety of new and used knives and firearms. KTP released three limited-production dealer special knives from 1995 to 1996. They include 25 serial-numbered Model 26 Pathfinders and 50 serial-numbered Model 25-5 Trappers with black Micarta handles and nickel silver hilts. Additionally, KTP produced 50 serial numbered Model 4-6 "Big Game and Skinner" hunters with desert ironwood handles.

L.L. Bean of Freeport, Maine, is no longer a Randall dealer. However, in the 1990s, L.L. Bean did sell serial numbered Randall Model 26 Pathfinders, each with an L.L. Bean blade etch and a stag handle. The L.L. Bean Dealer Special has a 4-inch high-carbon steel blade and is 8.25 inches long. There were 375 L.L. Bean Dealer Specials produced.

The Shaw-Leibowitz Dealer Special was marketed as "The Lewis and Clark Commemorative" knife in the 1970s, with a blade etching commemorating the Lewis and Clark Expedition. The goal of the dealer/maker collaboration was to produce 300 etched knives, but only 144 pieces were made. Each sports a 6-inch carbon steel blade with a Model 6 style grind, rosewood handle, nickel silver guard, and a duralumin butt cap. The overall length is approximately 11 inches, and the accompanying leather sheath has "LS" stamped on the back.

When Shaw-Leibowitz ceased production at 144

knives, Randall dealer Jack Crider acquired the remaining 156 blades and had them finished with different handles, but they were not etched. The Springdale, Arkansas, knife purveyor A.G. Russell Knives has been an authorized Randall dealer since 1986. The original A.G. Russell Dealer Special was first sold in 1996—a 4-inch drop-point skinner with a stag handle and a compass on the end. In 1997, the design was changed to incorporate a stacked leather handle with brass and black spacers. There apparently was an offering of this model, in 2007, with a desert ironwood grip.

The Massive Sasquatch

Randall dealer Doug Kenefick of Connecticut introduced the Randall Made Knives Sasquatch model in 1978. With a design influenced by the knifemaking styles of Rod Chappel and Gil Hibben, the Sasquatch is available in a choice of an 11-inch high-carbon steel blade or an 8-inch stainless blade. The 11-inch model is massive, with its cousin being the Randall Smithsonian Model 12 Bowie. The blade geometry incorporates kukri and Samba features, and it is the largest dealer special ever sold by a Randall purveyor.

Nordic Knives was owned by Dave Harvey and Bob Gaddis, with the latter writing the authoritative reference book on Randall Knives titled "Randall Made Knives, The History of the Man and the Knives."

The "Nordic Special," also known as the "Nordic Knives Drop-Point Special," was introduced in 1982 and discontinued in 1997. But, in 1999, it became available as a non-catalog Model 11-3 Alaskan

Skinner. In 1998, Nordic came out with a new Dealer Special called the "Nordic Special Bowie." Styled like the 19th-century English Sheffield bowies, it has a 7-inch, flat-ground stainless blade with the Randall logo stamped on the ricasso. The leather sheath is also stamped "Nordic Knives Special" around the Randall logo.

The late Jack Crider of Ohio was a Randall dealer for many years. The "Jack Crider Special," also known as the "Poor Man's Fighter," first appeared in 1983. The knife traces its roots back to the Model 10 Salt Fisherman knife. Unlike its predecessor, the Jack Crider Special is not hammer forged, but rather fashioned using the stock-removal method, including a choice of a 5- or 7-inch, full-tang stainless blade. Most models have saw teeth, slab handles of either Micarta or wood, and no guards, but instead wrist thongs. The sheath is stamped "Jack Crider Special."

Tom Clinton became a Randall dealer in the early 1970s and sadly passed away in August 2008. His son, Gary, has continued the legacy with Clinton Knives, the largest full-service Randall Made Knives dealer. The Clintons are some of the finest folks in the world of Randall Made Knives. In 1988, Tom introduced the "Clinton Special" featuring a 7-inch, 1.5-inch-wide, double-edge stainless blade, a slightly forward curving nickel hilt and a stamped ricasso. Handle materials vary.

Tom released a limited edition of 500 serial numbered "Vietnam Veteran" Model 14's with 7.5-inch stainless blades, finger-grooved green canvas Micarta handles and riveted roughback sheaths. The blades and sheaths are stamped "Vietnam Veteran." He also offered the Randall Made Knives African "Big Five" knife set. Each knife showcases a stainless blade etched "AFRICAN BIG FIVE," a white Micarta grip hand-scrimshawed by Ron Skaggs, and a special carrying case. This is the only multi-knife set ever made by Randall, and although limited to 100 sets, less than 60 were completed.

Model and scrim descriptions are as follows:

1) Model 3-5, scrimshawed elephant with a buffalo leather sheath
2) Model 25-5, scrimshawed lion with a crocodile leather sheath
3) Model 27, scrimshawed leopard with an ostrich leather sheath
4) Model 12-6, scrimshawed cape buffalo with a crocodile leather sheath
5) Model 23, scrimshawed rhinoceros with a zebra leather sheath

Captain Chris Stanaback of Sportsman's Services in Florida released his "Stanaback Special," in 1987. Options for the full-tang bowie include a 4- or 4 5/8-inch stainless blade with thumb notches and a top sharpened edge. The blade geometry is like a large Model 8 "Trout and Bird" knife. An oxblood leather

Of the limited-edition knives Randall dealer Tom Clinton released are a dealer special with a white Micarta handle, a "Vietnam Veteran" model, and the "African Big Five Knives," all from the Evan Nappen collection.

Rick Bowles was Randall's official scrimshander and a Randall dealer since 1988. His "RBS" dealer special was influenced by the Green River Skinner knives of the 1800s.

sheath stamped "Capt. Chris Stanaback" comes with a distinctive EZE-Lap diamond sharpening steel in a front tube pouch.

Until it permanently closed its doors, Stoddard's Inc. of Boston was the oldest continuously operating knife shop in America, dating back to the year 1800. Stoddard's offered a dealer special called the "Sergeants Model" based on the Model 19 5-inch Bushmaster with a sunburst-style briarwood handle. Later models could be ordered with a desert ironwood handle. Each knife marked "Stoddard's, Inc" above "Boston, MA SN. #XXX" has a dull false edge because of the Massachusetts law banning double-edged knives.

Passing away in February 2023, Rick Bowles was Randall's official scrimshander and a Randall dealer since 1988. His "RBS" dealer special was influenced by the Green River Skinner knives of the 1800s. Each serial numbered Randall Made Knives RBS model has a 5.5-inch blade etched "RBS," with many pieces unsurprisingly sporting scrimshawed handles. Until 1993, sheaths for Bowles' Specials had the letters "RBS" stamped on the back, and after 1993, they read "Rick Bowles Special."

Wayne Buxton, of Garland, Texas, became a dealer for Randall Made Knives in the early 1970s. In 1994, he first offered the "Buxton Fighter," a bowie featuring a black Micarta "Border Patrol" handle, and a 6.5-inch blade with a full tang that extends beyond the end of the handle like the Vietnam-era Randall Model 14 with a "skull crusher pommel." Each serial-numbered blade is marked "B.F" and comes with a Model C sheath stamped "Buxton Fighter" around the RMK Logo.

The Andy Thornal Company is a world-class sporting and outfitter's store in Winter Haven, Florida, and has been a Randall dealer since 1969. The first version of the "Andy Thornal Special" debuted in 1974. It's like a 5" Model 12-6 Little Bear Bowie with a deep thumb notch and stag handle. One hundred knives were made, each marked "A.T.S." with a serial number, and the back of the sheath reads "Andy Thornal Special." A floral design is on the front of the sheath under the stone pocket.

The second A.T.S. resembles a Model 5-4 and appeared in 1977. One hundred were produced, and these, too, were marked and serial numbered. The third A.T.S. was a Model 26 Pathfinder with a Model 25 stag and stacked-leather handle and an inlaid coin reading "Andy Thornal Company, 50 Years" to celebrate the Florida company's 50th Anniversary. There were 150 marked and numbered knives made beginning in 1995.

Over the years, the Randall Knife Society (RKS) has offered its own Special Edition Knives. The following descriptions come from the legacy website of the RKS, RandallKnifeSociety.com:

• **RKS1 - First Club knife**

In 1991, RKS offered a fighting knife featuring a 5-inch blade, brass and blue spacers, a brass double hilt, and a choice of a black Micarta handle with black Model A sheath or a stag handle and brown Model A sheath. Etched on the reverse side: "RKSA Serial # / Member #." There were 564 stag-handle knives and 436 black Micarta pieces produced for a total of 1,000 RKS1 knives.

The "Buxton Fighter" features a black Micarta "Border Patrol" handle and a 6.5-inch blade with a full tang that extends beyond the end of the handle.

The fourth Randall Knife Society Club Knife came with either a stag handle and nickel-silver double hilt or leather handle and brass hilt or guard.

• RKS2 - Second Club knife

This knife was offered to the membership in 1995. There were 338 Micarta-handle knives and 298 stag models made. Each knife has a 4.5-inch blade etched with "RKS Serial # / Member #."

A round 1/2-inch-diameter brass RKS shield is inlaid in the butt of the stag handle.

The black Micarta version has aluminum and black spacers and a Border Patrol handle with a duralumin crow's beak butt. The single hilt is nickel silver, and a round 1/2-inch-diameter RKS silver shield is inlaid on the front side of the handle. The RKS2 models came with RKS-stamped Sullivan sheaths.

• RKS3 - Third Club knife

This knife was first offered in 1997. There were 860 knives made. It's a slightly smaller version of the Randall 50th Anniversary Commemorative Knife with a total of 17 spacers. The stag handle has a 9/16-inch RKS medallion in the butt, and the RKS3 comes with a Sullivan sheath.

• RKS4 - Fourth Club knife

This knife either had a stag handle and nickel silver double hilt or a leather handle and a brass double hilt. Gary Randall calls it the Model 4-8" Fighter. A customer sent in an old model of this knife for repairs. Gary said he knew the Model 4-8" Fighter

existed after seeing a picture of the movie star Robert Taylor wearing one in a World War II photo. There were 1,200 RKS4 knives sold. Of these, 816 had stag grips and 384 were leather-handle versions.

• RKS5 - Fifth Club knife

The fifth RKS knife was a miniature drop-point hunter. There were 1,500 knives made and offered in 2006 to members of RKS only. Each sported a black Micarta handle, brass guard, stainless blade, and a Sullivan sheath stamped with the Randall logo "M" stamp.

Early Randall miniature knives were uncommon, and there are many fakes. Legitimate, more modern miniatures have been produced, including the Model 25 in 1996, the Model 1 in 1998, and the Model 3 in 2000.

These first three miniature models were limited to a production run of 1,500 each and are serial numbered. The Model 14, in 2004, was limited to 3,000 serial-numbered knives. Randall added the Miniature Model 27 to the catalog, in 2012, and soon after the Copper Miniature Model 27. The Model 27 miniatures are not serial numbered and have no production limit. □

Sources

"Randall Made Knives – The History of the Man and the Blades" by Robert L. Gaddis, Paladin Press, 1993; "Randall Knives - A Reference Book by Sheldon & Edna Wickersham," Private Printing, 2007; and "Randall Dealer Special Knives" by Kent Harrison, RKS Newsletter #27, June 1995.

Miniature Randall Made Knives have been produced, including these two versions of the Model 25, in 1996.

POLISHING *Japanese* SWORDS

How to make details of the steel surface come to life and tell their story.

By Leon Kapp

Takaiwa Setsuo sits in the traditional sword polisher's position on a classic *togi dai*, or work area. The floor is sloped to allow water to run away from the work area. *(Aram Compeau photo)*

*J*apanese swords have specific properties or characteristics, and on a properly polished sword, they should be readily visible to appreciate or study. The basic elements of a Japanese sword are the shape, the *jigane* (steel surface details, color, and texture), and the *hamon*, or outline of the hardened zone—the temper line.

The shape should have a clean and uniform curved surface, flat back surfaces, and flat upper faces or sides (if those are present). All the lines should be clear and sharp, and appropriate surfaces should be rounded or flat.

The steel surface or jigane should not be bright or reflective, but somewhat dark, and details of the steel's surface should be at least partially visible. These details include features such as the *jihada*, or visible pattern created on the blade's surface from the repeated folding and hammering out of the steel during the process going from raw steel (*tama hagane*) created by a traditional Japanese smelter (*tatara*) to the final steel used in the sword.

The pattern could be prominent and clear, or tight and barely visible. This depends on how old the sword is, where in Japan it was made, the quality of the *tama hagane*, and the forging methods used. The steel used in a traditional Japanese sword never melts in the smelter during refining or repeated heating and hammering to draw it out.

In general, the steel in a sword is folded about 12 times for most swords, but this can vary depending on the quality of the original starting material and the smith's tradition. This process means that there will not be a featureless and bright surface on the sword. Details may be hard to discern, but with good polish and lighting, many will become visible.

The hamon is made when the sword is covered with a complex insulating clay coating composed of two types and then heated and quenched in water. The edge region cools rapidly and is converted to martensitic steel while the body of the sword remains in ferrite and pearlite forms. With traditional polishing methods, the martensitic hamon becomes visible and contrasts with the ferrite and pearlite body of the sword.

Polisher's Skill

Exactly how much contrast there is between these two regions depends on the polisher's skill and judgment, as well as on the individual sword and its condition (how it was heat treated and annealed, and if it was polished many times, etc.). There are several details within the hamon area. The boundary between the ji and hamon is called the *nioiguchi*, and there can be many complex structures in that area. With good polishing, these fine details or structures should be visible.

There may often be martensitic or hardened areas in the ji above the nioiguchi, and these can be very helpful in dating and placing the maker of a blade, so a good polisher's goal is to make these details clear if they are present.

What does the polisher have to do? The polisher's goal is to finish and refine the shape of a new sword, or to restore an old sword to its proper and optimal condition. Because of the features of the sword, that means the polisher wants to have a clear and well-defined shape with the appropriate regions being flat or curved, sharp lines, and with a properly shaped and defined point.

There should be a clear and fine surface on the ji with details of the jihada and color visible, and martensitic features in the ji (above the hamon or nioiguchi) visible if they are present. The hamon should be well-defined and the nioiguchi should be clear. Fine details on the inside of the hamon, as well as the nioiguchi, should be visible. The hamon

The stone is held in position by the polisher's foot over a wooden clamp, or *fumaegi*. Natural polishing stones are brittle and can fracture if clamped in place too strongly, and a fumaegi clamp gently holds the stones in place. Additionally, the stones are interchanged often, and it is easy to change them with this arrangement. *(Aram Compeau photo)*

Natural polishing stones: The dark-blue stone on the far left is uchigmori jito, and the light grey one next to it, uchigumori hato. The stone on the far right is kaisei. *(Aram Compeau photo)*

should be clearly visible and in contrast with the ji.

The back surface (*mune*) and upper flat part of the blade's surface (*shinogi ji*) should be flat and smooth and will have a final appearance produced by burnishing those surfaces with a series of steel burnishing needles, or *migaki bo.*

All areas are polished using natural stones, but today some modern synthetic stones are used as well. In the past, the earliest stages of the polishing process were performed using only natural stones, and some polishers today still use only natural stones.

Ara Togi, or Foundation Polishing

Japanese sword polishers use natural stones, but today synthetic stones are employed in the earliest stages. The initial stones used in the polishing process are called (in order of increasing fineness) *arato, kongoto, binsui, kaisei,* and *nagura.* Today, these are usually modern synthetic stones. The abrasive particles in modern stones are extremely fine, and more importantly, uniform.

With traditional natural stones, especially in the early polishing stage using rougher stones, abrasive particles are not completely uniform, and one will occasionally polish over a large abrasive particle and leave a deep scratch on the blade.

It takes a lot of time to polish, stone by stone, using rough natural stones, and to completely remove all the scratches from the previous stone before progressing to the next. As a result, it is faster and produces better results to use a series of modern stones for the first six or seven polishing stages.

The uniform particles of modern stones make it faster to finish each stage of the polishing process and progress to the next stone. These stones are readily available in Japan, and manufacturers continually offer new ones with various abrasive particle sizes and differing degrees of hardness.

The last synthetic stone used is called nagura, and results with it are comparable to those obtained using its natural equivalents. After this stage, the stones used are *chu nagura, koma nagura, suita* (with many grades), *uchigumori hato,* and *uchigumori jito.*

Hamon Becomes Visible

After using the last synthetic nagura stone, the hamon outline is usually just visible, and possibly some traces of the jihada or surface pattern can be discerned. Polishers will begin the natural stone series with nagura or suita, depending on how the blade appears after using a synthetic nagura.

Usually after using the natural nagura, the hamon boundary or nioiguchi becomes crystal clear and the steel surface or ji starts to become much smoother looking and uniform. This process continues with several progressively finer suita stones (usually two or three increasingly fine suita stones are used). After using the suita stones, the nioiguchi is clear, the steel surface becomes darker and uniform, and traces of the jihada appear over the entire blade.

Following the suita stones, uchigumori-hato is used, and work with this stone is somewhat concentrated on the top of the hamon area or the nioiguchi. This makes the hamon details and structure of the nioiguchi extremely clear.

The last large stone used is uchigumori-jito, and the focus of this stone is on the ji. The jihada should be visible at this stage. More than one uchigumori-jito stone can be used depending on the appearance of the sword.

This means that, in general, five synthetic stones are employed, and sometimes up to seven in this group. Up to seven natural stones might be used with several stones of one type. These are nagura (none or one or two), suita (one to three), uchigumori hato (one or two), and uchigumori jito (one or two). The exact number of stones employed will depend on the sword and how careful or ambitious the polisher wants to be, as well as the exact outcome he or she wants to see.

Time-Consuming Process

As a result, this is a time-consuming process, and not all swords are polished with as much effort. Exactly how a sword is polished depends on the sword, polisher, and what he or she wants to make visible in a final polish. At each stage when polishing a sword with natural stones, a polisher might test two or three similar stones before progressing and polishing the entire sword with a specific one.

In theory, modern abrasive stones should be capable of completely polishing a Japanese sword. However, there are two properties of polishing stones that are critical: one is the fineness of the abrasive material used, and modern materials appear to be sufficient in this respect. The second property of the stones is their overall hardness.

The abrasive particles are held together in the form of a stone by some type of matrix or material that provides its shape and supports the abrasive particles. The material used to hold, shape, and form modern synthetic polishing stones is extremely hard and far harder than traditional natural Japanese suita and uchigumori stones. As a result, fine abrasives in modern synthetic stones have no effect above the nagura stage stones (with a grit number of approximately 2,000 or higher).

Continuing to work with modern stones past this stage simply equates to buffing or burnishing the steel, resulting in a bright, almost featureless surface (although the hamon outline may be visible). Consequently, it is necessary to finish the polishing process with natural stones to see a traditional appearance in a polished Japanese sword.

There are many sources of natural stones in Japan, and they have been quarried all over the country for at least 1,500 years. Most uchigumori stones are found in the Kyoto area, however, a polishing stone was recently discovered in a 1,500-year-old dolmen, or tomb, in Japan with a polished sword. So, there is some information and a sample available of the earliest polishing materials.

Shiage Togi, or Finish Polishing

Once a polisher has finished with the large stones, there are still more steps required to produce a satisfactory traditional Japanese polish. Even the finest polishing stones leave very minute marks or traces on the steel, and these must be removed at the next stage of polishing.

After the last polishing stone is used, the polisher goes over the blade with a fine stone, called a hazuya, made from uchigumori-hato stones. In preparing *hazuya* from the large uchigumori, the stones are split into thin slices. The slices are covered with lacquer, then the lacquer is covered with fibrous Japanese paper or washi, and the stones are ground down to a thin paper-like wafer.

The stones are cut into small pieces about 0.5 inches to 0.75 inches in size, and the polisher uses his thumb to move them over the entire blade. This removes the last marks from the uchigumori stones and helps make the jigane or steel surface and

The last stones used are hazuya and jizuya. They are backed with lacquer and Japanese paper, ground thin, cut into oval shapes, and used for the last polishing steps. Takaiwa Setsuo is cutting a hazuya into an oval shape for use in polishing the hamon. The black pieces seen in the background are the back sides of lacquer-covered hazuya stones, and the visible black surfaces are urushi lacquer. Japanese paper *(washi)* is embedded in the black lacquer, thus holding the thin stones intact. *(Aram Compeau photo)*

Takaiwa Setsuo uses a burnishing needle to polish the shinogi ji, or the upper flat surface of a new sword made by Yoshindo. The hamon outline is clear and complex, and there will be a dark mirror-like finish on the shinogi ji when it is done. *(Aram Compeau photo)*

hamon details clearer.

After using the hazuya stones, another type of harder stone called *jizuya* is prepared in the same manner. These stones are split off from an uchigumori-jito stone and backed with lacquer and washi paper like the hazuya stones. The uchigumori-jito stones are harder and finer than the uchigumori-hato, so the jizuya stones can produce a finer finish and are used over the entire blade. The jihada can become crystal clear at this stage. Generally, more than one of these jizuya stones will be used.

The next step is to go over the entire blade yet again with nugui. There are two types of nugui. One is sashi-komi, which is prepared from well-ground black iron oxide suspended in clove or choji oil. Another, kanahada, is prepared from well-ground red iron oxide suspended in clove or choji oil. The nugui is rubbed over the entire blade under a piece of cotton. Generally, the blade color will become darker and have a uniform appearance after a nugui treatment.

Finish the Hamon

The second-to-last polishing step is to finish the hamon, emphasize its appearance and contrast it with the ji or body of the blade. This is done by preparing a *hadori* stone. Basically, the hadori stone is a thin wafer of uchigumori-hato backed with lacquer and paper like the hazuya stone. The polisher will select soft pieces of uchigumori-hato stones to use for the hadori, since softer hazuya stones will more easily whiten the hamon.

The stones are cut into oval shapes, and the polisher works with each one under his thumb to whiten or emphasize the hamon. The polisher must be careful to faithfully follow the hamon's shape. Good work with the hadori stone will highlight the hamon, emphasize its actual outline and shape, and make it visible against the ji or body of the sword.

Excessive work and whitening with the hadori stone can result in a hamon that almost appears to be painted white and can obscure fine and characteristic details inside of it that should be visible and are part of the sword's nature or character.

The final polishing step involves burnishing the back surface (mune) or the flat upper sides (shinogi-ji) of a shinogi-zukuri-style sword. This is done by going over the surfaces with one of several shapes of steel burnishing needles.

Polishing the blade with uchigumori stones has a strong effect on the final appearance of the burnished surfaces. Therefore, surfaces to be burnished are polished with all the polishing stones described here before the burnishing step is performed.

Polisher's Position & Lighting

A Japanese polisher works in a traditional position sitting on a short stool (about 10 inches high) and on a sloped surface. Water is the only lubricant used to keep the stones clean, and a lot of water runs off the stones onto the sloped floor of the polishing area, or *togi dai*. This position is important, because a

In examining this tanto by Yoshindo's brother, Shoji, the jihada has a fine, even, and uniform appearance. There is a dark grey color, and the hamon is a simple, straight suguha style. The hamon's nioiguchi is a narrow, straight line and is visible in the photo.

This closer view of the tanto by Shoji reveals that the jigane has a fine, tight, well-forged, and uniform grain pattern visible over the entire blade. It is called a fine *itame hada*, or wood grain pattern. The hamon is a simple, straight suguha pattern.

sword is heavy, and the polisher's shoulders must be over the sword he or she is working on to carefully control its angle and position over the stones.

Lighting is important in polishing and examining a sword. Since a sword is made from high-carbon steel, it is relatively bright and extremely reflective. Because very bright light makes it difficult to discern fine details on a Japanese sword, lighting in a Japanese polishing shop is usually subdued, and little direct outdoor light is allowed into a polishing area.

There is usually a point source of light such as a small halogen bulb or LED light in front and/or positioned to the side of the polisher, and at an angle of 45 degrees to the blade. It is unknown how swords were viewed, or details visualized, in the past, but historical books from the 16th century describe all the fine details we look for today on a sword.

Some historical references suggest that a hole was made in a *shoji* panel (door or window), and the hole was positioned so that the sun came through it during part of the day. This would have created a strong point source of light that likely would have allowed a skilled polisher to visually examine all the details we look for in a sword today.

The Finished Sword

If a quality sword is polished by an experienced polisher, the ji should have a dark color that allows details of the jigane such as the steel surface pattern, or jihada, to be visible in places, if not everywhere. The strength of the jihada and the pattern itself can provide information on not only the age of the sword but also the smith. The hamon should be clear, and fine details (if present) in the hamon should be visible. Any visible detail helps to provide information about the smith and the age of the sword.

The upper surfaces (Shinogi ji) should be flat, uniformly burnished, and have a dark color. The curved surfaces should be smooth and uniform, and the final appearance of the surface of the ji and hamon uniform over most of the sword.

Not all polishes are the same, and sometimes one sees a sword with a featureless surface on the ji, a bright and reflective surface, an undulating (rather than flat) shinogi ji, and a hamon that is extremely white and in which no fine details can be discerned. The appearance and polish of each surface must contribute to the overall appearance of the sword and allow fine details of the steel and hamon to be visible. If a sword is poorly polished, it will be difficult to appreciate it and learn about its origin.

Polishing is a difficult skill to learn, and most Japanese polishers are students and apprentices for about five years or more before becoming independent. In Japan, there is a national competition held every year in Tokyo for new swords and polishing and other sword-associated crafts. Prizes are awarded for sword making, polishing, and other skills, and can lead to recognition and promotion of the best craftsmen and newcomers in each field. □

A modern tanto fashioned in the 1930s by Hideaki, in Hokkaido, is made from traditional tama hagane. The jihada is a visible and straight *masame hada* surface pattern. The hamon is a *suguha*, or straight hamon.

A *koto katana*, a katana made before 1600 A.D., was built by Kiyomitsu, who worked in Bizen Province in the mid-1500s. The steel is dark and the jihada is a strong and prominent *itame hada*, or a wood grain pattern. The hamon is complex and the nioiguchi, or boundary, shows gunome loops, *yahazu*, or tadpole-like choji loops, and some low *gunome*, or simple loops. There are parallel, almost straight white lines just below the nioiguchi, called *kinsuji*. The shinogi ji, or upper flat surface, is burnished, but the prominent jihada is visible on the burnished surface.

The Kitchen Knife as a Survival Blade

Can a butcher knife persevere when put to the test in wilderness survival situations?

By James Morgan Ayres • All images by ML Ayres

The Old Hickory Sticker made quick work of splitting palm tree bark to be used as kindling.

an a kitchen knife serve as a survival blade? Well, I have used kitchen knives for that purpose on several occasions. So have many others. I grew up on stories about how one of my ancestors served with Rogers' Rangers and others had come through the Cumberland Gap with Daniel Boone into Kentucky. I was fascinated by those anecdotes and raided the public library and country museum where I found books about Boone and Davy Crockett, as well as other accounts of early settlers. The books told stories of Indian raids or about natives and settlers living side by side.

I read that long hunters, 18th-century explorers and hunters who made expeditions into the American frontier for as much as six months at a time, carried "long knives." Having always been drawn to the blade, learning about long hunters motivated me to dig deeper. Eventually, I discovered that the "long knives" used by Boone, Crockett and others were simply quality butcher knives with lengthy blades about 7-12 inches apiece. Some were hand forged by local smiths, others imported from England. These knives were used for dressing game, camp chores, and as weapons … in essence, survival knives.

With a long-bladed butcher knife, a tomahawk, muzzleloading Kentucky rifle, bag of *rockahominy* (rough-ground cornmeal), pemmican and a blanket roll, they survived and prospered for extended periods in the wilderness the likes of which no longer exists in America.

In my imagination, I wanted to be a long hunter or an Indian. I had read "The Last of the Mohicans" about Hawkeye and Chingachgook. I was 10 years old and figured either one would do as a role model. I set out to equip myself for wilderness adventure as a long hunter. First, of course, I had to have a long knife.

There was a butcher knife in our kitchen with an 8-inch blade. I measured the blade and decided it would do for my long knife. It had been my grandfather's and had what I now know was a carbon steel blade. Grandpa didn't like "shiny knives that won't take an edge." It had wooden slab handle scales and a flat-ground blade that would slice ham so thin you could see light through it. Over Mom's repeated objections, I claimed it.

Grandpa taught me proper, safe knife handling. He made a sheath for it from some old leather and encouraged me in my pursuit. I set up a wood target in the backyard and practiced throwing that knife until I could stick it on a half-turn, whole-turn, or no-turn. Hey, Boone threw knives and tomahawks, right? So did Spencer Tracy in "Northwest Passage."

I couldn't convince myself that Grandpa's heavy hatchet was a tomahawk, so I took to the woods near our house with as close as I could get to the long hunter's outfit—my long knife, a blanket roll Mom put together, some corn cakes and cracklings. Those Midwestern woods were a century from the real wilderness, but deer, rabbits, squirrels, raccoons, foxes, and other critters lived there. The streams were filled with fish. The forest was big enough to get lost in. Some kids did.

Forays into the Woods

I made many expeditions to that "wilderness." Well, it was wilderness to me. I never encountered any Indians or other hostiles, so never had to use my long knife as a weapon. I did, however, use my long knife

A 10-inch chef's knife is used to gather juniper boughs for a fragrant bed.

The 10-inch chef's knife and Sabatier utility knife are shown on a hunting bag.

A Sabatier utility knife is employed to fashion a fishing spear.

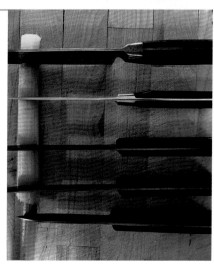

From top to bottom are a 10-inch chef's knife, Sabatier utility knife, Old Hickory Sticker, Old Hickory Hunting Knife, and Old Hickory Fish and Small Game Knife, all full-tang models with steel running the lengths of their handles.

(Mom's kitchen knife) to split wood for kindling, and clean fish and small game, which I took with my bow and deadfall traps I made using the blade. I also cut river cane for shelters, cattails for bedding, ripped open dead logs for dry wood in rainy weather, and in short, used it for everything for which a wilderness survival knife could be employed. I even took a rabbit with it once by standing still against a tree trunk until the bunny came within throwing distance. That might sound like a tall tale, taking a rabbit with a thrown knife, but it's a true story. And on a good day, I can still throw a knife that well, more than a half-century later. I can still get close enough to wild game to almost touch them, too.

Much later, I got off the bus from Fort Benning, having completed jump school at Smoke Bomb Hill, home to Special Forces. The first person I saw on my arrival at Training Group was a sergeant wearing a Green Beret and a big knife on his belt. A few days later, he told me his knife was a Randall. Randall knives had a legendary reputation in Special Forces. He let me handle his knife and said, "Son, get yourself a Randall. It can save your life." I did. It did. That's another story.

That Randall redefined for me what a survival knife should be. I carried and used it in survival

An Ontario Knives Old Hickory Hunting Knife strips dead bark from a palm tree for tinder.

The author uses a Sabatier chef's knife to downward beat (or baton) a bowie knife.

schools and on deployment. I learned that it would do anything that needed to be done in the jungle and mountains, support my weight, cut through a helicopter skin and an auto body, and do other things that would not have been possible with my old, long knife. Clearly, it was superior to the old butcher knife in many ways. That said, I recall other occasions when kitchen knives did serve as survival knives … within their limits. Kitchen knives are not hard-use knives.

A guy who became a good friend showed up at Fort Bragg with an Old Hickory Sticker, including a double-edge carbon steel blade, full tang, and wooden handle slabs. Mike was an Inuit, lived close to the earth and had used that knife for everything you can use a knife for, including fighting seals that tried to steal his fish. Mike never went for a Randall; they cost almost a month's jump pay. The Sticker was his tried-and-true survival knife that he figured would continue to work for him. As far as I could tell, it did.

Many years later at Winter Count, a gathering of primitive skills teachers and students, I met Albert Avril, an Apache who was one of the instructors. Albert's everyday all-purpose survival knife was also an Old Hickory Sticker. I asked him why he chose that knife. The most popular knife in that crowd was the Mora. He said, "The Mora's a good woodcarving knife. I have one. But it's no survival knife. A survival knife must do anything you need it to do."

Albert kept one edge razor sharp for meat cutting and other fine work, and one edge with a thicker bevel for woodwork and rough use.

Once when I was in France, while traveling through the Auvergne and staying in small village inns, I decided to go for a walk for a few days in the country's largest national park. There, small groups of stone houses have been abandoned and become ghost villages. Deer step delicately through the green woods and wander along broken and unused roads. In mountain passes, eagles soar at your fingertips, close enough to touch, it seems, in the clean icy air. Crumbled castles and ruins from Roman times add to the mystery and beauty.

Old Hickory Hunting and Small Fish and Game knives are pictured with leather sheaths.

A Wild Boar Bush Knife?

A friend who hunted this area warned me about wild boar, large, red-eyed, mean-tempered wild boar that will attack a human if they're feeling cranky. I had only a folder. I needed a bush knife. It's a comfort to have a foot of good steel in the night when the winds howl, and unseen creatures thrash through the darkness, especially wild boars. In a village store, I found a heavy, 10-inch Sabatier chef's knife, forged in one piece with handle scales riveted in place, strong and durable to stand up to the demands of professional use. The original design was from a medieval dagger and served as a tool and weapon in days gone by.

The old knife had been used and neglected. The blade was rusty, dull, and pitted. But it balanced well in my hand and felt like it could be trusted. I bought it, along with a small, thick plastic sheet, the kind used for covering cutting surfaces, a roll of tape, and a sharpening stone. When warmed over a fire, cut

to size, shaped around the blade, and secured with a couple of layers of tape, the plastic sheet made an effective sheath for the big blade. A good scrubbing with an abrasive kitchen cleaner removed the rust. A few minutes with the stone put a ferocious edge on its carbon steel blade.

With my Sabatier tucked into the back of my belt and a few supplies in my small rucksack, I was ready for the woods. It was a measure of my confidence in the Sabatier that I felt equipped to deal with a boar if it came to that. As it turned out, I didn't have to fight a wild boar with my Sabatier. Its actual utility was limited to slicing venison from a village shop, getting some kindling, and a few other mundane tasks. But I was glad to have it.

Over the years, I have used that same chef's knife to make river cane shelters, as I did when a boy with Mom's butcher knife, and for general field use. I've also used it to test survival and combat knives with hard beats to their spines. If a knife billed as a

An Old Hickory Fish and Small Game Knife sharpens a spear point.

survival or combat knife won't take a beat from my Sabatier, I discard the broken shards.

During the past 20 years or so, I've done field reviews on hundreds of knives, probably over a thousand, for BLADE Magazine. They include forged knives made by American Bladesmith Society master smiths and other bench-made and custom blades, and factory survival knives. Combined with years of field use, I've acquired a pretty good idea of what works. Heck, I wrote a book on survival knives (https://www.amazon.com/Survival-Knives-Choose-Right-Blade/dp/1510728422.)

So, if a kitchen knife can do the job of a survival blade, what's the point of spending hundreds of dollars on specialty knives? Performance. Both a Honda and a BMW will do 100 miles an hour. But the Honda will be on the ragged edge of its performance envelope, whereas the BMW will be well within its design limits. A kitchen knife won't perform like a forged blade from a master smith. Nor will it stand up to the hard use that some well-made factory and custom survival knives can handle.

But for much wilderness survival use, they'll do, especially if you have a good kitchen or butcher knife and know how to use it. Ontario now offers a few of its Old Hickory knives with leather sheaths that, combined, are set up for outdoor use. We employed each of the Old Hickory models, along with other kitchen knives for field use. All performed well. Henckels International and Victorinox also make good, solid kitchen knives that will handle wilderness survival tasks at a modest price. Most Sabatier (a maker's mark used by several kitchen knife manufacturers) models are considered high-quality pieces that suffice as survival knives.

If you think you might need to rip open a fire door, cut through helicopter skin, pry open the door of a wrecked auto, dig out from a collapsed building, or punch through body armor (all things people have done with knives to survive), you would be better served with a hard-use knife such as those made by Fallkniven, Spartan Blades, TOPS Knives, DPx Gear or any one of dozens of makers of quality survival knives, or with one made by a custom cutler. But for wilderness survival use, a good kitchen knife can do what needs to be done. □

Victorinox and Sabatier kitchen knives are suitable for woodcraft and wilderness survival.

Hard-use, non-kitchen survival knives include, from left to right, the Spartan Blades Enyo, DPx Gear HEST, TOPS Travelin Man 2 and the Fallkniven A1.

TRENDS

L ast year, there were so many pictures of handmade cleavers submitted for the *KNIVES* book, I was convinced they would compose an emerging and expansive trend. This year, there were some beauties submitted, but not as many.

Just when I thought I had seen every style, model, and pattern of knife in existence, including all the historical, exotic, and ethnic pieces imaginable, Jim Cooper submitted an image of knifemaker Collin Maguire's custom clinch pick model. I am somewhat embarrassed to admit, I had neither seen nor heard of clinch pick knives, but not only are they out there, several makers seem to use them as inspiration for their own blades, sans the sharpened spines and with edges on the bellies of the blades. Yet the sizes and shapes of the everyday carry and utility knives are eerily similar to clinch picks (now that I know what they are).

The point is that predicting trends in knives is like forecasting the weather or beating the stock market. It is an inexact science, and if one could perfect it, he or she could retire tomorrow with money in the bank. Speaking of money, check out the "Money Micarta," "Capital D-Guards" and "Boujee Bowies" on the following pages, and where did the "Abundance of Bog Oak" come from?

All the knives within the Trends section of the book are "money," fashionable, classic, the crème de la crème, clean, beautiful, and, of course, trending. These are the blades that keep the industry moving forward and progressing so new enthusiasts and buyers come on board and immerse themselves in a world of handmade blades.

Cleaver Creations

« CODY ADOLPHSON:
Apocalyptic mango was a sweet choice for the handle of a 1084-and-15N20 san mai blade complete with an 80CrV2 core and a nickel silver bolster. *(Jocelyn Frasier photo)*

» MIKE and AUDRA DRAPER:
The "MAD Cleaver" cuts the mustard via a shark's tooth pattern damascus blade, integral guard, blackwood handle, and mosaic pins. *(SharpByCoop image)*

《 CHRIS GREEN:
The cleaver has looks that kill, including features like a dyed redwood burl handle and a 7-layer clad-damascus blade with a 1080 core. *(Jocelyn Frasier photo)*

》 JOSHUA FISHER:
It doesn't get much beefier than a meat cleaver in an antiqued 8670 carbon steel blade and a red canvas Micarta handle. *(BladeGallery.com photo)*

» LUIZ GUSTAVO GONCALVES:
A hand-forged 11-bar Turkish twist-pattern damascus blade gets things cracking on a meat cleaver that also features a hand-sculpted African blackwood handle and gold inlays.
(BladeGallery.com photo)

« MARDI MESHEJIAN:
If the Inconel 8 1095 blade is as sharp as it looks, the roast will be sliced in no time. That's a Goncalo Alves (tigerwood) handle, too.
(SharpByCoop photo)

Abundance of Bog Oak

Why is there so much bog oak on knife handles nowadays? Did someone clear-cut a bog of all its ancient oak trees? That's not so far-fetched, but let's back up a minute. First off, you don't clear-cut ancient trees—they fell thousands of years ago. But there is renewed interest in retrieving or harvesting the oaken logs that have been submerged in bogs for several centuries or even millennia.

After so many years spent immersed in oxygen-poor, acid-rich bogs, swamps, or muddy riverbanks, the tannic acid in the oak has reacted with the iron salt in the water, strongly discoloring the wood, turning it into something extremely hard, dark, and rich in history. The wood color ranges from light gray to yellow, brown, and deep black.

Bog oak is often found in regions that used to have large bogs or swamps, such as Central Europe, for example, where moors were still common in the Middle Ages. The trunks of bog oak used today are up to 8,500 years old, making bog oaks subfossil structures. They are the remains of once-living organisms that are not fully fossilized yet.

Now knifemakers are turning bog oak into high-quality handles. There's an abundance of the ancient wood, and knife users and collectors are the blessed bog oak beneficiaries.

» BILL OGDEN:
The mini-axe is the lucky recipient of an Alabama Damascus double-bit head, a nickel silver guard, and a 5,400-year-old bog oak handle. *(SharpByCoop photo)*

« SASHA ROSENFELD:
A chef's knife exhibits an 8-inch san mai blade, stabilized ancient bog oak handle, and stainless bolster.
(BladeGallery.com photo)

« KYLE HANSON:
The hunter is outfitted in a W2 blade and 5,600-year-old bog oak handle scales. *(SharpByCoop photo)*

« DAN TOMPKINS:
The damascus-core san mai chef's knife is served up in an ancient bog oak handle with a red resin spacer and mosaic pin.
(Caleb Royer photo)

» DERRICK WULF:
The multi-bar twist damascus blade is a winsome addition to the vest bowie in a bog oak handle. *(SharpByCoop photo)*

» TYLER HACKBARTH:
Go-Mai damascus makes up the business end of a short sword featuring a fluted ancient bog oak handle with nickel silver spacers. *(Jocelyn Frasier photo)*

Great Honed Hunters

« CLARENCE DEYONG:
Not your average hunter in a red stag handle, this one's a canister steel masterpiece with a twist damascus guard, and a woolly mammoth ivory spacer and pommel.
(Mitchell D. Cohen Photography)

« CHRIS GREEN:
The ram's horn-handle hunter with W1 blade and forged, integral guard will outlast this and many lifetimes before entering the happy hunting ground beyond.
(Jocelyn Frasier photo)

« RODRIGO ENGLERT:
An integral, forged hunting knife sports a 5160 blade in a Brut de Forge finish, mammoth ivory handle scales, and a braided leather thong. *(Caleb Royer photo)*

« SHAYNE CARTER:
Done up in a feather damascus blade, and damascus guard, ferrule and pommel, the stag-handle hunter stretches 9 7/8 inches overall.
(SharpByCoop photo)

» BEN AKIN:
The small, compact, and lightweight belt knife makes for a nice EDC/hunter in a hand-forged 52100 blade and ironwood handle scales.
(BladeGallery.com photo)

⌄ MARK SCRIMGEOUR:
The 3.625-inch CPM 3V blade of the Carolina Reaper is heat treated with Delta Protocol and complemented by a black Micarta handle. *(SharpByCoop photo)*

« H.L. HOLBROOK:
The CPM 154 hunter features a tapered tang, red spacers, stabilized curly oak handle slabs, and a mosaic pin.
(Eric Eggly/PointSeven photo)

⌃ BILL BEHNKE:
Hemp wood is an inspired choice for the handle of a damascus hunter that includes a patinated bronze guard and a laminated phenolic spacer.
(Mitchell D. Cohen Photography)

⌃ CODY HOFSOMMER:
With a .38 Special shell planted in the butt of the stag handle, the ladder-pattern damascus hunter also features a ringed Gidgee spacer and a bronze guard.
(Cory Martin photo)

LIN RHEA: The master smith was mindful of great hunting knife design in fashioning the 80CrV2 model with sheep horn handle and stainless hardware.

(Jocelyn Frasier photo)

» ARNO BERNARD: A little bird-and-trout knife in a satin-finished Bohler S35VN blade and stabilized bird's-eye maple burl handle is calling your name.

(BladeGallery.com photo)

» EDDIE STALCUP: The black paper Micarta bolster is grooved to match the stag handle of the CPM 154 hunter. *(SharpByCoop photo)*

» RYAN SIMON: A red-dyed sassafras handle with black G-10 liners was a nice choice for the W2 tool steel hunter. *(Rod Hoare photo)*

« E. JAY HENDRICKSON:
The wire-inlaid wood grip won't
slip, and the blade will stay true.
(SharpByCoop photo)

» TOM PLOPPERT:
A CPM 154 lock-back
folding Arkansas hunter
wears its exhibition-grade
ebony handle scales with pride.
(Mitchell D. Cohen Photography)

⌃ RYAN BREUER:
A 1080 drop-point hunter with integral bolster is
fitted with an heirloom-quality buckeye burl handle.
(BladeGallery.com photo)

⌃ MIKE MACINNES:
A forged 5160 hunter enlists a brass
guard and butt cap, sambar stag handle,
and G-10, Micarta, and brass spacers.
(Cory Martin photo)

⌃ JESS HOFFMAN:
The maker gave the CPM Magnacut
hunter a "tuxedo look" via carbon-fiber
handle scales and resin ivory bolsters.
(Cory Martin photo))

« JIM POLING:
True knife enthusiasts can appreciate clean integral hunters in W1 blades and walnut handles. *(Mitchell D. Cohen Photography)*

« JON MOORE:
The coyote jaw handle and random pattern damascus blade have equal parts bite.

⌃ TOM BUCKNER:
Ancient wooly mammoth ivory and a laddered W's-pattern damascus blade make up the bulk of a Bob Loveless-style dropped hunter. *(BladeGallery.com photo)*

⌃ WILLIE VAN DER MERWE:
The field skinner is largely hand-ground M390 stainless steel and contoured amboyna burl. *(BladeGallery.com photo)*

» GAETAN BEAUCHAMP:
A Catherine Chabot painting of predator and game graces the water buffalo horn handle of a stainless damascus hunter.
(Eric Eggly/PointSeven photo)

⌃ MARCUS LIN:
This hot little Ultralight Hunter is forged from Takefu Yu-Shoku steel and sports a black linen Micarta guard and desert ironwood handle.

(SharpByCoop photo)

⌃ PAT BIGGIN:
The damascus hunter has a brass guard, stacked leather spacers, and a naturally beautiful handle.

(Cory Martin photo)

⌃ NEAL GREEN:
A fixed blade trapper is outfitted in a Magnacut blade, Micarta handle, G-10 spacers, and titanium hardware.

(Jocelyn Frasier photo)

« MARK SINCLAIR:
Stabilized bone adheres to the full tang of the "Swagman" CPM 154 fixed blade via mosaic pins.

(Rod Hoare photo)

» ANDERS HOGSTROM:
Antiqued bronze and stag make a nice combo on a 1050 high-carbon skinner with wispy hamon (temper line).

(Mitchell D. Cohen Photography)

BRION TOMBERLIN:
The Little River Hunter is dressed in a hand-forged 1084 blade and a stabilized curly Koa handle.
(BladeGallery.com photo)

JORDON BERTHELOT:
The straight skinny on the carved leaf skinner is that it has an HHH Valkyrie damascus blade, a textured nickel silver guard, a turquoise spacer, and a white G-10 handle.
(Caleb Royer photo)

BENNETT SNIPES:
This great honed hunter is a 1095 drop-point example with a bronze collar and desert ironwood body.
(SharpByCoop photo)

SCOTT HALL:
The CPM S35VN hunters come in clip- or drop-point blades, and red/black G-10 or stabilized maple burl handles.
(Cory Martin photo)

» RUSTY WAIDE:
The damascus hunter comes in a combination bog oak, True Stone, carbon fiber, and mammoth ivory handle.
(SharpByCoop photo)

⌃ JARRETT CIESLAK:
Dressed in a stabilized and dyed curly maple grip, the clip-point hunter conducts business via a hand-forged W1 high carbon steel blade showcasing a Japanese clay zone heat treatment. *(BladeGallery.com photo)*

» DAVID KELLEY:
Buckeye burl handle scales enliven a mid-size W2 hunter with black liners.
(Mitchell D. Cohen Photography)

« CORY MARTIN:
The 1095 integral hunters are given a Cerakote finish and hand-carved titanium overlays. Each comes with a Kydex sheath (not shown).
(Cory Martin photo)

《 JOE MANGIAFICO:
The "Brook Trout," "Brown Trout,"
and "Rainbow Trout" models come
in Nitro-V blades, brass, Micarta,
and mokume-gane guards, and
G-10, copper, and brass handles.
(SharpByCoop photo)

》 WESLEY WERNIMONT:
Check out this winsome hunter
in a flat-ground W2 blade,
stainless guard, and
purpleheart wood handle.
(Mitchell D. Cohen Photography)

》 RICK KEMP:
A small hunter is delivered in
a flat ground 15N20 blade,
a Wandoo wood handle,
and mosaic pins.
(Rod Hoare photo)

《 SHAWN ELLIS:
Dinosaur bone is befitting
of an integral damascus
hunter that comes with a
hand-stitched, pouch-
style leather sheath.
(BladeGallery.com photo)

« PEDRO GONZALEZ:
A tastefully assembled hunter includes an AEB-L stainless blade, a resin-based white Juma bolster, and a combination of Koa wood and Raffir Noble composite handle scales.
(BladeGallery.com photo)

« RIAN DOUDLE:
The classy "Raven" utility hunter sports a multi-bar damascus blade, bronze guard, and Turkish walnut grip.
(Rod Hoare photo)

« ADAM MILLE:
Crown stag, vintage Micarta, and copper make up the handle half of a W2 hunter.
(SharpByCoop photo)

« KELLY FRASIER:
A copper guard complements the masur birch handle and 80CrV2 blade of a Yak Mountain Hunter.
(Jocelyn Frasier photo)

❥ JOHN SCHULTZ:
A 120-layer twist-damascus hunter with a stainless bolster, and aluminum-bronze guard is a true treat.
(Mitchell D. Cohen Photography)

≫ HENNIE DU PLESSIS:
The damascus hunter is treated to copper flake carbon-fiber handle scales set on a full tang.
(BladeGallery.com photo)

« BUTCH DEVERAUX:
In the style of Ed Fowler, the clip-point buffalo hunter dons a convex-ground 52100 blade, a brass guard, and sheep horn handle. *(SharpByCoop photo)*

« DEON NEL:
Details like textured stainless bolsters and a hand-carved Arizona desert ironwood handle elevate the Bohler N690 drop-point hunter to the next level.
(BladeGallery.com photo)

« DOUGLAS NOREN:
A William Scagel-style hunter is treated to a satin-finished 5160 carbon steel blade, and a stacked leather, black and red fiber, mammoth ivory, and ancient walrus ivory handle.
(BladeGallery.com photo)

« WILL STELTER:
With a wide "Twisted W's" damascus blade and long fossil walrus ivory handle, the hunter is a handsome and handy piece of equipment. *(SharpByCoop photo)*

Capital D-Guards

« HARVEY DEAN:
A master class in classic D-guard making and engraving, the bowie sports a "Texas Wind" pattern damascus blade and ancient ivory handle.
(SharpByCoop photo)

« JAMES EMMONS:
While mammoth ivory scales and a hot-blued D-guard make up the handle half, the business end is 11.5 inches of ladder W's damascus.
(Jocelyn Frazier photo)

« DAVID LISCH:
A stag-handle D-guard bowie is the beneficiary of a "Mystic Butterflies" mosaic damascus blade and domed gold spacer.
(Eric Eggly/PointSeven photo)

« MACE VITALE:
An antique bowie reproduction, the Lilac is no wallflower, but a steel and stag stud.
(SharpByCoop photo)

On-Point Slip Joints

« BOBBY HOUSE:
Amber European stag, a hand-engraved houndstooth shield, and checkered liners highlight a CPM 154 slip joint with a long nail pull. *(Eric Eggly/PointSeven photo)*

« JIM DUNLAP:
The marvelous mammoth ivory handle scales of the sowbelly stockman can't even be outshined by the clean CPM 154 blades. *(Mitchell D. Cohen Photography)*

⌃ TOBIN HILL:
The grand undertaking involved fashioning a six-blade, hollow-ground sowbelly pocketknife with amber stag handle scales. *(SharpByCoop photo)*

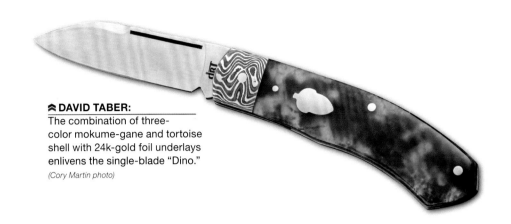

DAVID TABER:
The combination of three-color mokume-gane and tortoise shell with 24k-gold foil underlays enlivens the single-blade "Dino."

(Cory Martin photo)

GEORGE BAARTMAN:
Lava flow carbon-fiber set on titanium liners sets a hollow-ground M390 slip joint in motion. *(BladeGallery.com photo)*

TANNER COUCH:
With a wide CPM 154 blade and long nail nick, the folder is dressed in natural stag, threaded bolsters, and a federal shield.

(Eric Eggly/PointSeven photo)

《 ADAM ROGERS:
The bent gunstock handle of the hollow-ground, random-pattern damascus slip joint is jigged bone. *(Rod Hoare photo)*

⌃ NICK TIMPSON:
The two-blade CPM 154 folder parades box elder burl handle scales and a singular handle shield.
(SharpByCoop photo)

⌃ CHRIS TAYLOR:
The maker's Nessie slip joint is executed here in a san mai blade, blue mammoth ivory handle scales, and titanium liners.
(Mitchell D. Cohen Photography)

⌃ BRUCE BARNETT:
Shark's tooth-pattern damascus and mammoth ivory pretty up a slip joint trapper.
(BladeGallery.com photo)

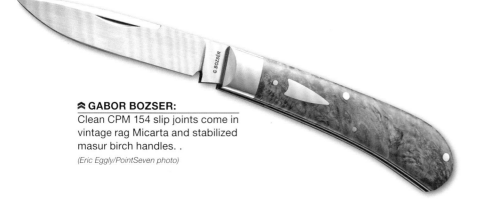

⌃ GABOR BOZSER:
Clean CPM 154 slip joints come in vintage rag Micarta and stabilized masur birch handles. .
(Eric Eggly/PointSeven photo)

CHRIS SHARP:
A damascus slip joint folder encourages the combined practices of families sitting on the porch strumming the guitar and whittling. *(SharpByCoop photo)*

BOB MERZ:
An elongated nail nick spans the spine of the CTS-XHP stainless blade on a jigged bone-handle slip-joint folder. *(BladeGallery.com photo)*

STEPHEN VANDERKOLFF:
A Dellana Dot grip system helps open the CPM 154 blade of a blue/green mammoth ivory-handle slip joint folder. *(Caleb Royer photo)*

NATHAN RAPTIS:
Nice things come in A2 tool steel and Chechen wood packages.
(Eric Eggly/PointSeven photo)

⌃ RYAN FORREST:
A single-blade slip joint folder
features a forest-green G-10 handle.
(Eric Eggly/PointSeven photo)

« TIM ROBERTSON:
The three-blade CPM 154 folder
sports integral stainless bolsters
and liners, and stag handle slabs.
(SharpByCoop photo)

« TOM PLOPPERT:
Right on point is a cattle knife with
CPM 154 blades and springs, integral
stainless liners and bolsters, and
antique Boker bone scales.
(Mitchell D. Cohen Photography)

» KEITH JOHNSON:
A gent's pocketknife is elegantly executed in a CTS-XHP blade with a long nail nick, a stainless frame and bolsters, and walrus ivory handle scales. *(SharpByCoop photo)*

⌃ MATT COLLUM:
The arching lines of a two-blade slip joint encompass CPM 154 blades, red stag handle scales, and a federal shield.
(Eric Eggly/PointSeven photo)

⌃ EVAN NICOLAIDES:
The "Workhorse" and "Snook" slip-joint folders parade CPM 20CV blades and springs, and roofline jigging on the handle scales.
(Mitchell D. Cohen Photography)

LUKE SWENSON:
Slip the four-blade, stag-handle
Case 54047-inspired folder into the
pocket for safekeeping until needed.
(SharpByCoop photo)

RICK NOWLAND:
Raindrop damascus and bark
mammoth ivory team up for the
good cause of a finely crafted
slip-joint folder.
(BladeGallery.com photo)

MATTHEW PARKINSON:
A stunning slip-joint
pocketknife is executed in
damascus and maple burl.
(SharpByCoop photo)

DAVID R. (D.R.) DAVIS:
Enter the slimline slip joint
in a stainless damascus blade,
black-lip mother-of-pearl handle
scales, 18k-gold highlights, and
jeweled titanium liners.
(Mitchell D. Cohen Photography)

Edges of the Earth

I was recently looking at the flags of all 254 countries. Why? Because that's what nerds do, of course. I did feel a bit square, to be honest. Anyone who is a fan of the television series "The Big Bang Theory" likely remembers episodes devoted to Sheldon and Amy's podcast "Fun with Flags." But I digress. The real reason I was casually studying the flags of all countries is that I like the artwork and symbols that the citizens, or at least the leaders and decision-makers at the time, chose to represent their country. It interests me.

That's a big undertaking if you think about it—how best to represent an entire country via a flag. Similarly, knifemakers who dabble in the patterns of different countries tend to take their jobs seriously. I've never met a maker who built exotic patterns half-heartedly. No, knifemakers are a perfecting bunch, and if they're going to reproduce another country's signature blade, they do it to exacting standards.

Such is the case with the "Edges of the Earth" herein, each a representative example of a people and culture in some part of the world, and their work and leisure activities that require the use of an edged tool or weapons. Sheldon and Amy would think that's nifty.

» CHARLES "CHUCK" COOK:
A tight little tanto exhibits a 256-layer raindrop damascus blade and a stabilized maple handle.
(SharpByCoop photo)

« ANDERS HOGSTROM:
A 1050 high-carbon Hong Kong cutlass features a fossil walrus ivory hilt, textured sterling silver fittings, and a bronze guard.
(Mitchell D. Cohen Photography)

« ANDREW GEASLIN:
A 22-inch stretch of 1084 steel makes up the bulk of a Malay parang that also features a carved Brazilian hardwood handle and wrought iron guard.
(SharpByCoop photo)

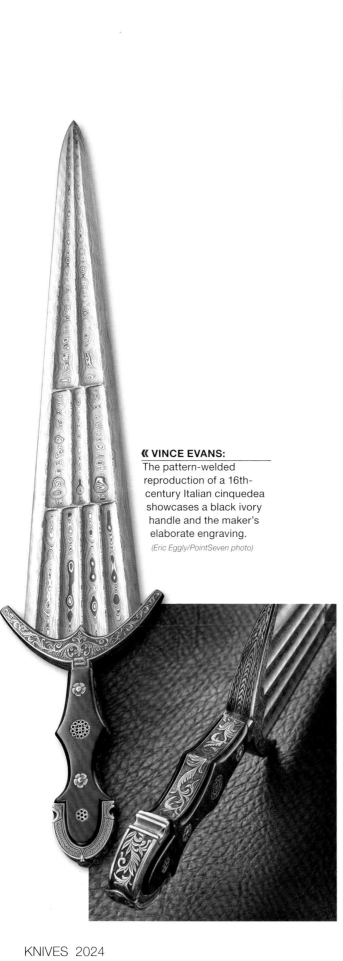

« VINCE EVANS:
The pattern-welded reproduction of a 16th-century Italian cinquedea showcases a black ivory handle and the maker's elaborate engraving.
(Eric Eggly/PointSeven photo)

« CARL MICHAEL ALMQVIST:
Highly patterned are the Roger Bergh multi-bar damascus blade and snakewood handle of the Nordic hunter.
(BladeGallery.com photo)

« JON MOORE:
The darkened hickory handle, brass tacks, and blued high-carbon steel head all give the Viking axe character.

« ALEX HOSSOM:
The maker takes liberties with the ancient Greek Kopis design, or modernizes it, here in a CPM 154 blade and Hawaiian Koa handle.
(Mitchell D. Cohen Photography)

« SCOTT SWEDER:
The Celtic leaf blade and the bronze guard will make one homesick for the old country, but the claro walnut brings it back to California.
(SharpByCoop photo)

« JARRETT CIESLAK:
Taking its blade shape cues from the Filipino karambit, the claw-like steel is hand forged 52100 in a satin finish, accompanied by a stabilized and dyed redwood burl grip.
(BladeGallery.com photo)

CHARLIE ELLIS:
The maker's rendition of a higonokami traditional Japanese folding pocketknife includes a damascus blade, and an antiqued 4130 chrome alloy steel handle.
(BladeGallery.com photo)

NEELS VAN DEN BERG:
A traditionally styled khanjar dagger, which traces its roots to Oman and the Middle East, features a "Shattered Glass" blade, a wood handle, and laser engraving by the maker.
(SharpByCoop photo)

DAVID MIRABILE:
The Hira-Zukuri tanto does the Samurai proud with a 13-inch W-2 blade and a cord-wrapped handle.
(SharpByCoop photo)

BERTIE RIETVELD:
The "Pugio [Roman dagger] Legacy2" leaves its mark in nebula damascus, black jade, Picasso marble, and Jonathan Knoesen engraving.
(SharpByCoop photo)

CH'IEN TURNER:
Slip this W-pattern damascus Saxon-style seax into your sash, allowing the South African red ivory wood handle to stick out a bit for appearances.
(BladeGallery.com photo)

《 ANDREW SMITH:
The head of the pipe tomahawk is forged from a 16-ounce ball peen hammer, sanded to a 400-grit finish, and affixed to a curly maple haft.
(BladeGallery.com photo)

《 ANDREW BLOMFIELD:
The handsome 5160 and desert ironwood gaucho knife sports a keyhole-style guard.
(SharpByCoop photo)

《 NICK ROSSI:
Of the integral tanto ilk, this modern version sports a CruForgeV blade, black linen Micarta handle slabs, and red liners.
(Mitchell D. Cohen Photography)

《 STEVE HILL:
In the style of a Spanish narvaja, the "Back in the Saddle" folder showcases carved swordfish bill scales and an abalone handle spine.

》 DERICK KEMPER:
Not your average Scottish dirk, the W2-and-15N20 damascus beauty boasts a dyed boxelder burl handle, silver guard, and engraving by Doug Brent.
(SharpByCoop photo)

Our Best Fighters

» STEPHAN FOWLER:
A finely fit and finished stag fighter showcases a four-bar twist damascus blade.
(SharpByCoop photo)

» ALEX HOSSOM:
The "Revenge Fighter" steps out in a wicked CPM 154 blade, curly maple handle, and black Micarta guard.
(Mitchell D. Cohen Photography)

» JORDON BERTHELOT:
The 11-inch carved fighter comes in swinging with a random-pattern damascus blade over an 80CrV2 core, sculpted and distressed nickel silver guard, and musk ox horn handle.
(Caleb Royer photo)

« ELIOTT ROBINSON:
This fly fighter exhibits a smoky temper line on its U10A high-carbon steel blade and a Tasmanian blackwood handle that won't quit. The knife comes with a Jeremy Guillaume leather sheath.
(SharpByCoop photo)

» WILLIAM TYC:
The Varn and Muckraker models waste no time transitioning from the Koa wood handles to the flat-ground CPM S35VN blades.
(SharpByCoop photo)

» KELLY VERMEER-VELLA:
While opponents try to figure out how the maker got the damascus pattern to match the blade shape, the mammoth ivory-handle fighter gets the upper hand.
(Eric Eggly/PointSeven photo)

» T.W. CHURCHMAN:
The file-worked full-tang 440C fighter is dressed in a Barasingha antler handle from Bandera County in the Texas hill country and jeweled stainless fittings.
(Caleb Royer photo)

« JOHN YOUNG:
The RWL-34 fighter was outfitted in a Picasso marble handle and that was all she wrote.
(Eric Eggly/PointSeven photo)

» BOBBY GARZA:
A chopper/fighter design is done in a san mai blade, paper ivory Micarta guard, and desert ironwood burl handle.
(Caleb Royer photo)

» DAVID LOUKIDES:
Fancy a fighter in 1084-and-15N20 damascus steel and an India stag handle.
(SharpByCoop photo)

« BUTCH DEVERAUX:
Fighters from Wyoming have convex-ground, triple hardened and tempered 52100 blades, brass guards, and sheep horn handles.
(SharpByCoop photo)

« CHARLIE ELLIS:
The forged 1084 armor-piercing Kwaiken enlists an epoxy-soaked, nylon cord-wrapped brown Micarta handle.
(BladeGallery.com photo)

» DAVID BROADWELL:
A double-ground, 600-layer damascus blade and Koa handle make up the bulk of the fine sub-hilt fighter.

(Mitchell D. Cohen Photography)

« ADAM MILLE:
A coffin-handle fighter is assembled from damascus steel and ironwood burl.

(SharpByCoop photo)

« ANDREW BLOMFIELD:
The framed-out sub-hilt fighter enters the ring in a 5160 blade and desert ironwood handle.

(SharpByCoop photo)

« FRANCOIS MAZIERES:
The bowie/fighter is fashioned from a forged-to-shape 1084 blade, and a stabilized quilted Tasmanian blackwood handle.

(Rod Hoare photo)

» MAVERIK MURDOCK:
A large, recurved fighter features a W2 carbon steel blade with smoky temper line and a natural Micarta handle.

(BladeGallery.com photo)

» SHANE MAGNUSSEN:
You might have to kiss something goodbye if you run across the AEB-L Kyss fixed blade with a carbon-fiber handle under the wrong circumstances.

(SharpByCoop photo)

« MARK SCRIMGEOUR and NATHAN CAROTHERS:
The HG Fighter is armed in a Delta 3V blade and a grooved Westinghouse Micarta handle.

(SharpByCoop photo)

« RYAN BREUER:
An integral keyhole fighter is no easy task to tackle, this example in a W1 blade and African blackwood handle.

(SharpByCoop photo)

» SPENCER REITER:
The CPM 154 fixed blades are part of the maker's "Hornet" series of stingers.

(Mitchell D. Cohen Photography)

« THEO NAZZ:
The 80CrV2 fighter has photovoltaic solar cells in the guard that power a small UV LED light inside the handle that also has a fiber-optic cable running through it to distribute light, so it always seems to be glowing faintly.

(SharpByCoop photo)

« PEDRO GONZALEZ:
The clay zone heat treatment of the W2 carbon steel blade is spectacular, as is the stabilized curly Koa grip of the fighter.

(BladeGallery.com photo)

« BUTCH DEVERAUX:
The Wind River Fighter sports a double-convex-ground 52100 blade, a nickel silver guard and North American elm burl handle.

(SharpByCoop photo)

» EDITIONS G:
Impeccably designed by Sam Lurquin, the Wardog2.0 enlists a full-tang 154CM blade and G-10 handle scales.

(SharpByCoop photo)

« DEON NEL:
Stabilized maple burl and textured bronze tag team for the handle half of a mirror-polished N690 fighter.
(BladeGallery.com photo)

⌃ TIMOTHY STEINGASS:
The trio includes Bob Loveless-style chute, dropped hunter, and boot knives in AEB-L blades and mother-of-pearl handles.
(SharpByCoop photo)

» KEVIN LESSWING:
The lines of the fighter, as well as those of the desert ironwood handle and temper line on the W2 blade are of equal impressiveness.
(SharpByCoop photo)

« BRIAN SELLERS:
Grab ahold of that musk ox handle and let the ladder-pattern damascus blade fly.
(SharpByCoop photo)

Harpoon-Style Blades

While you wouldn't want to jump ship with a harpoon bowie or fighter in hand to take down a whale as if it were a wild boar cornered by dogs (I'm not sure you'd want to do that, either), the blades herein are ferocious, or "lit," as my kids would say. And I found out that doesn't mean "lit up" or drunk, but rather legitimate. I think that was a few years back, so I'm probably behind again.

But I digress … not only is it surprising that there could ever be anything new in knives after epochs and eons of humans making them, but there seems to always be something new in knives. The latest happens to be harpoon-style blades with raised clips along the spines like the barbs on the lily irons of harpoons that prevent the arrow-like projections from coming out of the mammals once speared.

The harpoon clips of knives are more for looks than spearing, but they'd do the job in a pinch, and they put a little flare in the fold of the blade, perhaps catching a potential knife buyer's eye. The way things are going, there will be plenty of buyers for harpoon-style blades. I mean, they're ferocious and lit.

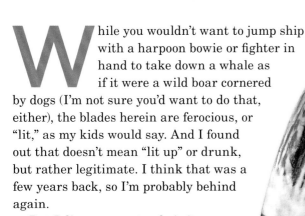

《 BOB EARHART:
The sloping sambar stag handle has as much character as the harpoon-style, feather-damascus blade, and that's saying something.
(SharpByCoop photo)

《 STEVEN RAMOS:
This whale of a knife features a 7.25-inch, recurved, mirror-polished, harpoon-style CPM 154 blade, dovetailed stainless bolsters, and icy blue sodalite handle scales.
(Caleb Royer photo)

« JAMES INGRAM:
Here's a mammoth ivory-handle flipper folder featuring a harpoon-style Mike Tyre feather damascus blade.

(SharpByCoop photo)

« EDWARD RATANUN:
A Damasteel tanto blade with a hollow harpoon clip makes up the business end of a P1 LinerLock including a Zirblast titanium handle and Damasteel underlays.

(SharpByCoop photo)

« EDMUND DAVIDSON:
Fully engraved by Jere Davidson, the harpoon-style Vixen CPM 154 fixed blade sports a Siberian mastodon ivory handle.

(SharpByCoop photo)

» J.W. RANDALL:
The feather pattern of the mammoth ivory-handle damascus fighter splays out perfectly into the raised clip of the harpoon-style blade.

(SharpByCoop photo)

Alloy'd Forces

The tactically elite: Blades built for the military and true tactical purposes hold a place of honor among the pantheon of edged tools and weapons. Knifemakers tend to take a bit more pride and care in fashioning knives that could be employed by our fighting men and women one day. And they should.

Outfitting the military is an honor reserved for the focused few, those who experiment with steel alloys to arrive at the right balance between a hard edge and a forgiving blade body. Knifemakers of service to soldiers put their efforts toward knife balance, sweet spots, utility, research into probable cutting chores and tasks, strong tips, perfectly honed edges, and overall tough steel blades.

Theirs is not a task to be taken lightly. If someone defending the rights and freedoms of their fellow countrymen needs to rely on their blade in a pinch, failure is not an option. Knifemakers I've met know this and take their jobs seriously. They are, after all, forging blades, removing stock, and designing, fashioning, and finishing knives for our Alloy'd Forces, and that's a heavy responsibility.

« TASHI BHARUCHA:
The "Die Hard" frame-lock folder features a bronze anodized titanium handle with speed holes, a zirconium spacer and collars, and titanium hardware.
(Mitchell D. Cohen Photography)

» BRIAN EFROS:
An overbuilt bolster-lock folder features a CTS XHP blade, canvas Micarta handle scales, and a four-alloy dark titanium pocket clip.

(Mitchell D. Cohen Photography)

» PAUL RASP:
A brass guard and pommel lend the Commando dagger some class, complemented by a leather handle and 7-inch AEB-L blade.

(Jocelyn Frasier photo)

« DEREK RAUSCH:
The Salvos survival knife dons a D-2 blade in a Cerakote finish, and an integral, round, hollow, diamond-pattern checkered grip.

(BladeGallery.com photo)

» CHUCK COOK:
The Open Range folder has a proper olive-drab G-10 handle, a titanium frame, and a saber-ground D2 blade.

(SharpByCoop photo)

» CASEY MIDDLETON:
The "Chupacabra" (legendary creature reported to have vampiric characteristics and drink the blood of livestock) frame-lock folder is built from a Nitro V blade, a zirconium frame on the show side and a titanium frame on the lock side, a zirconium pocket clip, and Timascus collars.

(Mitchell D. Cohen Photography)

« DUSTIN DRIVER:
The Havoc wreaks its namesake via a compound-ground Damasteel blade, titanium frame, and Micarta inlay.

(SharpByCoop photo)

» WILLIE VAN DER MERWE:
A Fairbairn-Sykes-style dagger incorporates a twist-pattern damascus blade, a heat-colored zirconium guard with 24k-gold inlays, and a contoured and antiqued bronze handle.

(BladeGallery.com photo)

« STEVE GATLIN:
Built for a female Marine Corps commander undertaking her first command, the Bob Loveless-style fighter exhibits a CPM 154 blade, stainless hardware, and a green canvas Micarta grip.

(SharpByCoop photo)

» JOE WATSON:
The large Kidon recurved fixed blade comes in choices of a W2 or 80CrV2 blade, and a stabilized Koa or cord-wrapped handle.

(SharpByCoop photo)

⩔ AARON WILBURN:
Created to be a no-nonsense workhorse, the "Bodyguard" belt knife features a 52100 high-carbon steel blade with Cerakote finish, and a natural canvas Micarta handle attached to a full tang via Torx fasteners.

(BladeGallery.com photo)

» TYLER HACKBARTH:
The sleek V-42-style stiletto sports a 53-layer twist-pattern damascus blade and a black and white ebony handle.

(JoeyAnne Meyers, Made By Design photo)

» RICHARD ROGERS:
Gun makers say frag pattern grips like on the Damasteel MUT folder are inspired by the MK II pineapple grenade used in World War II.

(Mitchell D. Cohen Photography)

» MARK SCRIMGEOUR and NATHAN CAROTHERS:
A full-tang, integral Delta 3V fixed blade enlists grooved double red Micarta handle scales.
(SharpByCoop photo)

» DANIEL KOERT:
Practically impenetrable materials include green canvas Micarta, zirconium, and CPM 154 blade steel.
(Mitchell D. Cohen Photography)

» JACKSON GROSE:
With a "Devastator" compound hollow-ground blade, the "Spiral 006" integral model features a black 550 paracord-wrapped grip.
(Rod Hoare photo)

« DAVID SHARP:
The matched set includes a tanto fixed blade and locking-liner folder in carbon-fiber handles and RWL steel blades.
(Mitchell D. Cohen Photography)

⌃ PRINCETON WONG:
The CTS 204P and titanium folder features a lock bar insert, hidden pivots, and full wraparound bolsters.

(SharpByCoop photo)

⌃ SCOTT HALL:
Users get a choice of CPM 3V steel with a black linen Micarta handle, or a partially serrated CPM S35V blade in a camo G-10 grip.

(Cory Martin photo)

⌃ LES GEORGE:
The U.S. 1918 MK1-style knuckle knife is delivered in a CPM S35VN blade, and a brass grip gorgeously engraved by David Riccardo.

(SharpByCoop photo)

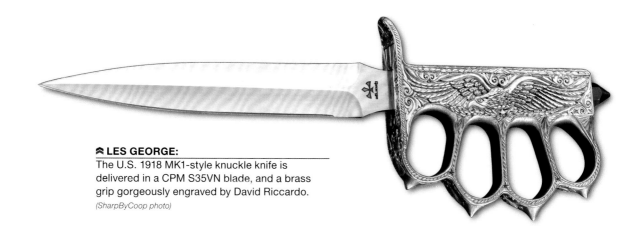

Biting
Behemoth Molars

Most ancient beings must be reconstructed by modern paleontologists from their bones. Not mammoths. Whole wooly mammoths have been found frozen in the permafrost of the Arctic, and thus, scientists know quite a lot about the ancient creatures. Preserved specimens with long hair have been discovered in Siberia, thus the "wooly" description, and mammoths once lived across much of North America and northern Asia.

Mammoths were generally taller than most of their Ice Age running mates, mastodons, and had longer tusks. Mammoth molars, like those used for knife handles herein, had broad, thin crowns with small linear ridges, somewhat like a giant file. Imagine that—knifemakers fashion old files or rasps into blades, so why not grips from mammoth teeth?

With the oldest mammoths dating back to the Pliocene Epoch 5.5 to 3.5 million years ago in southern and eastern Africa, the beasts came to North America in a series of migrations across a land bridge that existed over the Bering Strait between Alaska and Russia.

The mammoth molars themselves show their age—the elements have done wonders to them, hardening, cracking, and creating a kaleidoscope of colors and patterns that no one can emulate, though hard as he or she might try. No, the biting behemoth molars herein are each one-of-a-kind, like fingerprints, flower petals, and the very snowflakes that combined to build a frozen tundra and preserve mammoths for epochs and millennia.

« JAMES EMMONS:
Mammoth tooth makes a statement on a random-pattern damascus fighter with a plum-browned steel guard, and a titanium frame and fittings.
(Jocelyn Frasier photo)

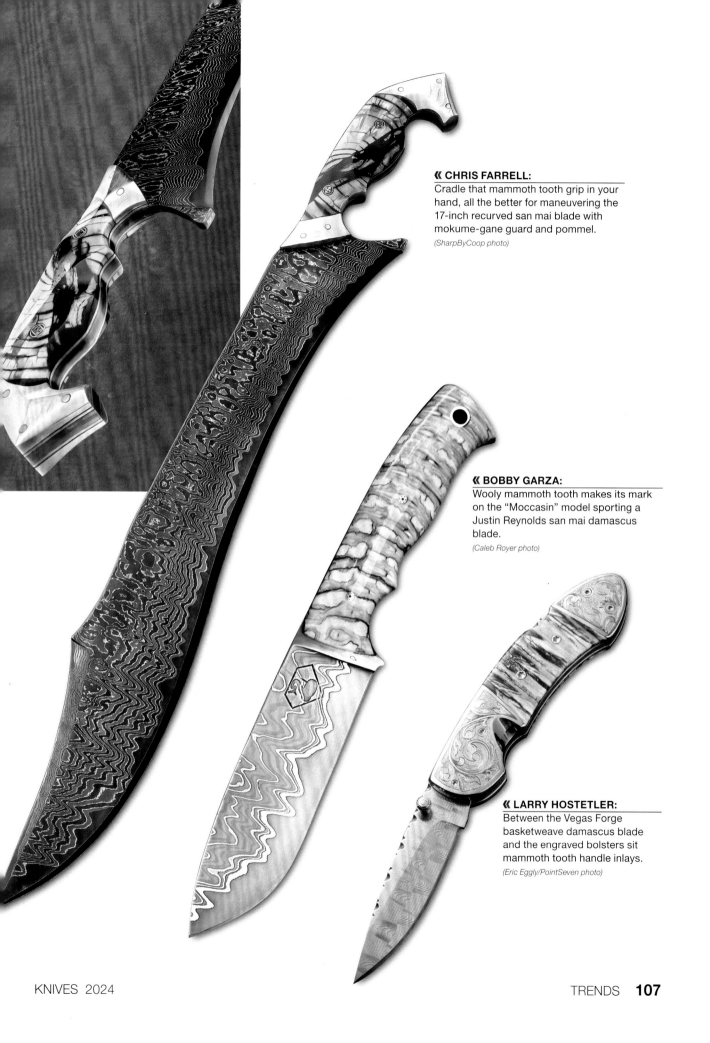

《 CHRIS FARRELL:
Cradle that mammoth tooth grip in your hand, all the better for maneuvering the 17-inch recurved san mai blade with mokume-gane guard and pommel.
(SharpByCoop photo)

《 BOBBY GARZA:
Wooly mammoth tooth makes its mark on the "Moccasin" model sporting a Justin Reynolds san mai damascus blade.
(Caleb Royer photo)

《 LARRY HOSTETLER:
Between the Vegas Forge basketweave damascus blade and the engraved bolsters sit mammoth tooth handle inlays.
(Eric Eggly/PointSeven photo)

⌄ ARNO BERNARD:
Mammoth molar lands the satin-finished Bohler S35VN utility/hunter in the trophy case.
(BladeGallery.com photo)

⌃ STEVE HILL:
Called "Winter Brook," the maker sees "a school of fish in the cold blue-green water" of the mammoth tooth handle, and possibly in the raindrop damascus blade of his Wharncliffe gent's folder.

» TREVOR BURGER:
Mammoth molar inlays bolster a Damasteel stainless damascus front flipper folder with carbon-fiber handle scales.
(BladeGallery.com photo)

» BRIAN MILINSKI:
Designed for an accomplished mineral collector, the damascus fixed blade parades a fossilized mammoth tooth handle, dovetailed water buffalo horn bolsters, and copper hardware.
(Caleb Royer photo)

« BOB MERZ:
Mammoth tooth adds further character to a CPM 154 lock-back folder.
(SharpByCoop photo)

Boujee Bowies

The high-class bowies on this and the following pages are classically styled with all the latest accoutrements—materials, steels, embellishments, and custom touches. They're not highbrow, but high-tech, more high-end than high and mighty.

Bowies are just as American as tantos are Japanese and puukkos are Finnish. They combine size and girth with controlled cutting, blending elements of butcher's knives with fighters, or camp knives with Spanish hunters. Steeped in history and lore, one is often indistinguishable from the other, adding mystery to the bowie knife.

They've come a long way from their butcher knife brethren of yore, and modern makers from the 1960s onward have perfected their craft. Some bowies integrate brass and copper into their makeup, others are forged from damascus, and still more exhibit ancient ivory, pique work, sculpting, texturing, and engraving.

These bowies are boujee. They're looking fine, dressed to the nines, working the crowd, and going around in all the right circles. Collectors are taking notice and paying bucco bucks for the boujee bowies. These are statement pieces speaking loud and clear.

≪ JASON FRY: The "I want to be Don Hanson when I grow up" bowie is forged from a 2-inch round bar of W2 steel, butted up against a browned mild steel guard, and handled in walrus ivory. *(SharpByCoop photo)*

≪ MILAN MOZOLIC: A nice, clean bowie blends an Arizona ironwood handle with an O1-and-15N20 Turkish twist damascus blade, and stainless hardware. *(Jocelyn Frasier photo)*

» JEFF HAINES:
An O1 bowie is executed in ironwood, brass, and mokume-gane.

(Mitchell D. Cohen Photography)

⌃ MICHAEL ANDERSSON:
The talented Swedish maker's take on a bowie includes a multi-bar twist damascus blade and a mammoth ivory handle.

(BladeGallery.com photo)

« ADAM MILLE:
Stabilized ambrosia burl and damascus vie for attention on a 10-inch bowie knife.

(SharpByCoop photo)

« MIKE MACINNES:
The spalted maple handle of the 5160 bowie is a tasty specimen.

(Cory Martin photo)

» SCOTT SWEDER:
With one of the finer feather-damascus blades in existence, the bowie combines it with a Gidgee wood handle, engraved hot-salt-blued guard, and blued pommel.
(Eric Eggly/PointSeven photo)

« BRUCE SCHUBERT:
The Australian knifemaker fashions a "Crocodile Dundee Bowie" in a 200-layer "Sunrise" ladder-pattern damascus blade, a brass guard, and stacked leather handle.
(Rod Hoare photo)

« ANDREW BLOMFIELD:
"Wandering Crosses" mosaic damascus makes its mark on a sub-hilt bowie with an ironwood handle and an engraved one-piece reverse keyhole-style guard.
(BladeGallery.com photo))

« JERRY FISK:
An "Arkansas Traveler" bowie hits the road in a "Dog Star" damascus blade, walnut burl handle, and some gold inlay and engraving for style points.
(SharpByCoop photo)

» BUTCH DEVERAUX:
A recurved, convex-ground 52100 Wyoming bowie represents the state in sheep horn and brass.

(SharpByCoop photo)

» DAWSON TABONE:
The mid-size 1085 bowie is built to last in a high mountain acacia handle, brass spacer, and stainless guard.

(Jocelyn Frasier photo)

» LEE PARSONS:
The bowie is brought to life in a "Texas Wind" damascus blade, brass guard, and black walnut handle.

(SharpByCoop photo)

« DERRICK WULF:
The bowie/fighter is brought to life in a damascus blade, titanium guard, and Gidgee wood handle.

(Mitchell D. Cohen Photography)

» ALEX YOAK:
The canister steel blade of the 16-inch bowie is forged from 52100 ball bearings and 1084 powdered steel and complemented by a European red stag handle from the Carpathian Mountain Range in Poland.

(Caleb Royer photo)

« BOB EARHART:
Don't tell the McCoys, but the Hatfield Bowie is a beauty, here in a 300-layer ladder-pattern damascus blade, sambar stag handle, and 1018 blued guard with hammered copper arrowhead overlay.

(SharpByCoop photo)

» PHILIP DUNN:
Turkish twist damascus and Karelian birch wood make for an eye-catching combination on a 16.7-inch bowie.

(BladeGallery.com photo)

« JAMES INGRAM:
And then there are the ones that just have bowie written all over them, like this frame-handle piece in 5160 steel, nickel silver, and ironwood.

(SharpByCoop photo)

« FOREST "BUTCH" SHEELY:
Some just know how to make the
damascus coffin-handle bowies sing.
(Mitchell D. Cohen Photography)

« TOMMY GANN:
The ABS master smith works one up in
hand-forged damascus, nickel silver,
and premium stag.
(BladeGallery.com photo)

» MIKE QUESENBERRY:
Turkish twist damascus steals
the show on a dog bone bowie
that boasts a fossilized walrus
handle with 18k-gold buttons and
escutcheon plates.
(SharpByCoop photo)

« ANDREW MEERS:
A 15.25-inch sub-hilt bowie enlists
a hand-forged, 800-layer damascus
blade, stag handle, and "Rose of
Sharon" gold inlay and engraving.
(BladeGallery.com photo)

《 RICHARD PATTERSON:
The fine 52100 bowie exhibits
a classic walnut handle.
(SharpByCoop photo)

》 LIN RHEA:
The bowie goes
boujee in a classy manner,
including a damascus blade,
fossil walrus tusk handle, and
stainless fittings.
(Jocelyn Frasier photo)

》 CHRIS BERRY:
A creative take on a coffin-handle
bowie blends a CPM MagnaCut
steel blade with a carbon-fiber
and silver twill handle.
(Mitchell D. Cohen Photography)

《 STEPHAN FOWLER:
The zebra damascus blade has
so much character, the koa-handle
bowie will always know company.
(SharpByCoop photo)

TYLER HACKBARTH:
Behold the bowie in a 21-layer, twist-damascus blade, ancient walrus ivory handle, wagon wheel wrought iron butt cap, and anchor chain and wrought iron guard with bronze spacers.
(Jocelyn Frasier photo)

TRAVIS WUERTZ:
A tribute to Tim Hancock, who passed away in 2019, the blade steel is named "Tim 94," and the bolster and guard are Hancock and Wuertz damascus.
(Mitchell D. Cohen Photography)

STEVE HILL:
The damascus and blue mammoth ivory model is inspired by an antique folding bowie.

SHAWN SHROPSHIRE:
A Pleistocene-era steppe bison bone handle anchors the 21-inch, 24-layer-damascus bowie that comes in a primitive rawhide sheath.
(SharpByCoop photo)

» JOEL WORLEY:
The splendid bowie blends a 1075-and-15N20-damascus blade with a carved walrus ivory handle.
(Mitchell D. Cohen Photography)

⌃ SAM BUTLER:
Stag and 5160 go a long way on a properly prepared bowie.
(SharpByCoop photo)

« MATTHEW PARKINSON:
The "Pradel" bowie is built from an 8-inch 1084 blade, sterling silver guard, and stabilized walnut handle.
(SharpByCoop photo)

» GARY RODEWALD:
The backcountry bowie relies on a forged W2 blade, stainless guard, and stacked G-10 and carbon-fiber handle, plus a bright-orange thong.
(BladeGallery.com photo)

« JIM POLING:
The maker's small bowie enlists a 4.25-inch, 74-layer twist-damascus blade, a red gum handle, and a steel hilt with a copper spacer.
(SharpByCoop photo)

Swords Drawn & Ready

《 BRENT STUBBLEFIELD:
Etched on each blade side of a Confederate mounted artillery saber reproduction are "Draw Me Not Without Reason" and "Sheath Me Not Without Honor."
(Caleb Royer photo)

SHEATH ME NOT WITHOUT HONOR

》 RYAN BREUER:
The bastard sword begins with a sculpted pommel cast from ancient bronze and treated with a hot patina, then segues into a leather-wrapped dogwood handle, and ends at the point of its 32.5-inch 8670 blade.
(SharpByCoop photo)

《 LIN RHEA:
European red stag anchors the clamshell-style D-guard sword with mild steel fittings and a 16.5-inch 80CrV2 blade.
(Jocelyn Frasier photo)

《 RON NEWTON:
A blackpowder gun/ knife combination, the kingly "Lion Sword" boasts a Turkish twist damascus blade, 18k-gold gun barrel, a sambar stag handle, O1 hot-blued miquelet lock guard and end fittings, and gold inlays and engraving.
(SharpByCoop photo)

》 ILYA ALEKSEYEV:
A spiderweb theme is carried out through the design of the double-edged mosaic damascus short sword with a wood, wire, and silver hilt.
(BladeGallery.com photo)

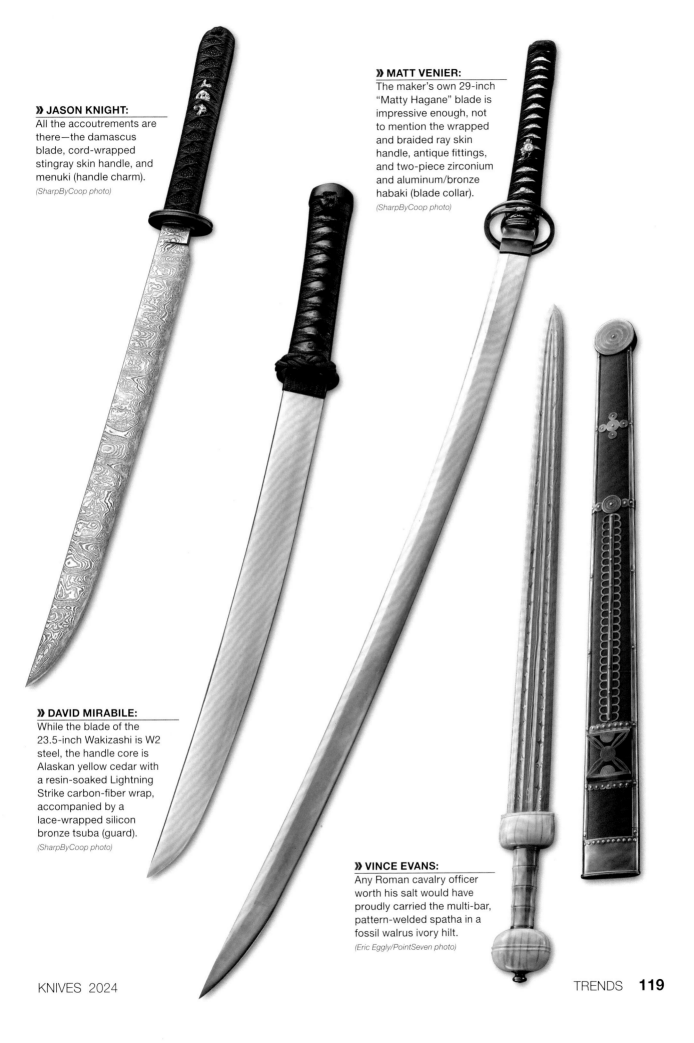

» JASON KNIGHT:
All the accoutrements are there—the damascus blade, cord-wrapped stingray skin handle, and menuki (handle charm).
(SharpByCoop photo)

» MATT VENIER:
The maker's own 29-inch "Matty Hagane" blade is impressive enough, not to mention the wrapped and braided ray skin handle, antique fittings, and two-piece zirconium and aluminum/bronze habaki (blade collar).
(SharpByCoop photo)

» DAVID MIRABILE:
While the blade of the 23.5-inch Wakizashi is W2 steel, the handle core is Alaskan yellow cedar with a resin-soaked Lightning Strike carbon-fiber wrap, accompanied by a lace-wrapped silicon bronze tsuba (guard).
(SharpByCoop photo)

» VINCE EVANS:
Any Roman cavalry officer worth his salt would have proudly carried the multi-bar, pattern-welded spatha in a fossil walrus ivory hilt.
(Eric Eggly/PointSeven photo)

» BRUCE SCHUBERT:
The 1,001-layer san mai blade of the clamshell cutlass features a 1084 core and is accompanied by a stabilized laced she-oak hilt.

(Rod Hoare photo)

« TOMMY CARROLL:
Chalking one up for creativity, the 1095 sword is handled in ostrich leg bone and comes with a sculpted serpent stand.

(Eric Eggly/PointSeven photo)

» ANDERS HOGSTROM:
"Book-matched complex mosaic W-theory damascus" by Joel Davis makes up the blade end of a bronze-handle falcata sword.

(Mitchell D. Cohen Photography)

« MARDI MESHEJIAN:
The damascus beauty boasts a Shibuichi (copper/silver) guard, fossil walrus ivory haft, and curly walnut scabbard.

(SharpByCoop photo)

Rosy Complexions

L ike walnut gunstocks, rosewood knife handles bespeak class and tradition. Plus, they add a little rosy hue to the mix of sharpened steel implements. The richly hued timber, often reddish-brown with darker veining, comes to knifemakers from Brazil, East India, Madagascar, Southeast Asia, Nicaragua, and other far reaches of the world.

Like the blades themselves, rosewood takes an excellent polish and is suitable for utilitarian and high art pieces. Many guitars, marimbas, billiard cues, fountain pens and chess pieces are fashioned from rosewood, and likewise furniture and luxury flooring. Rosewood oil is even used in perfume. Now most knifemakers will readily admit that there's nothing better than a rosy complexion and the smell of perfume.

» MYKEL PIPER:
Honduran rosewood stands out against stabilized bog oak and black and white carbon fiber on the handle of a Mega Mek utility knife.
(SharpByCoop photo)

» BRIAN MILINSKI:
The "Outback" bird-and-trout knife features an Alabama Damascus blade, and Honduran rosewood handle scales with mosaic pins.
(Jocelyn Frasier photo)

⌃ RYAN BREUER:
A hand-forged, recurved camp knife is treated to an 80CrV2 carbon steel blade and a Siamese rosewood grip.
(BladeGallery.com photo)

⌃ BEN PITTMAN:
Honduran rosewood is the handle material of choice for the utility hunter in a 5-inch 1084 blade, and combination stainless and nickel silver guard.
(SharpByCoop photo)

⌃ SAM REED:
With an 8.5-inch hand-forged V-Toku2 san mai chef's knife in the kitchen, such as this in a rosewood grip, everything's wine and roses.
(BladeGallery.com photo)

Classically Styled Folding Knives

⌃ TONY BAKER:
Hand-rubbed CPM 154 blades and nephrite jade handle inlays highlight the interframe stockman.

(BladeGallery.com photo)

⌃ DAVID TABER:
The triple-blade whittler pattern might be classic, yet the Corvette Fordite handle material is anything but, nor are the Carbo Quartz bolsters.

(Cory Martin photo)

« TOBIN HILL:
The sweet little swing-guard lock-back folder is hollow ground steel and solid stag.

(SharpByCoop photo)

« DAVID TUCKER:
An interframe slip-joint trapper benefits from mammoth bark handle inlays and a Nitro V blade with a mokume-gane (copper and nickel) jacket.

(Rod Hoare photo)

P.J. TOMES:
A "Baby Bullet" mid-lock folder showcases a satin-finished 12C27 stainless blade, and stag bone handle scales.
(BladeGallery.com photo)

TANNER COUCH:
A fine CPM 154 folder features a natural stag handle, fluted and threaded bolsters, and a houndstooth shadow line around the shield.
(Eric Eggly/PointSeven photo)

ADAM ROGERS:
The "Half Congress" folder features hollow-ground, ladder-pattern damascus blades, a CPM 154 spring, stainless bolsters, and hunter-green jigged bone handle scales.
(Rod Hoare photo)

DAVID R. (D.R.) DAVIS:
An AEB-L stainless four-blade congress pocketknife sports pearl-inlaid mammoth ivory handle scales, gold accents, and file-worked liners.
(Mitchell D. Cohen Photography)

JEFF HAWKINS:
A Tony Bose Lanny's Clip-style folder is executed in Doug Ponzio damascus, stainless steel, and mother-of-pearl.
(SharpByCoop photo)

TOMMY GANN:
A Coke bottle slip joint folder is executed in a 52100 blade with a hand-rubbed finish, black Micarta, and stainless steel.
(BladeGallery.com photo)

« MICHAEL VAGNINO:
A "Lanny's Clip"-style back-lock folder parades a Chad Nichols stainless damascus blade and a jigged and heat-colored titanium handle.

(BladeGallery.com photo)

⌃ DON HANSON III:
In a fat penny trapper style, the knife parades ancient mammoth ivory handle scales, a W2 tool steel blade, and a stainless shield, liners and pins.

(SharpByCoop photo)

⌃ KEITH R. JOHNSON:
A two-blade CTS-XHP tail-lock example comes in stainless bolsters and mammoth ivory handle scales.

(Cory Martin photo)

» MARDI MESHEJIAN:
A pair of damascus Wharncliffe folders fare well in mammoth ivory and fossil walrus ivory handles, the latter with carbon fiber thrown in, and copper lock bars.

(SharpByCoop photo)

» BRUCE BARNETT:
A saddlehorn lock-back folder enlists CPM 154 blades and Arizona desert ironwood handle scales.
(Rod Hoare photo)

« CHRIS SHARP:
In a classic pattern with beautiful damascus blades, stag handle scales, and the maker's patented inlaid handle shield, it hits all the right notes.
(SharpByCoop photo)

⌃ TYLER TURNER:
What you do is outfit the lock-back whittler with interior mammoth ivory handle scales so that the textured stainless bolsters stand out more.
(Eric Eggly/PointSeven photo)

» DANIEL KOERT:
A Persian blade shape is incorporated into the modern locking-liner folder that also employs Chad Nichols Boomerang damascus, zirconium, and titanium.
(Mitchell D. Cohen Photography)

⌃ BOB MERZ:
The maker fashioned a mid-lock folder incorporating a CTS-XHP stainless blade and African blackwood handle scales.
(BladeGallery.com photo)

⌃ TOM PLOPPERT:
The maker's rendition of a
Remington 1306 lock-back
folder involves a CPM 154 blade,
pre-ban ivory handle slabs, and
a stainless bullet shield.
(Mitchell D. Cohen Photography)

⌃ TIM ROBERTSON:
There's nothing quite like a
stag-handle lock-back whittler
designed just right.
(SharpByCoop photo)

⌃ BILL RUPLE:
Sometimes a guy just gets a
hankering to make an elephant
toenail folder in amber stag and
CPM 154 steel.
(Eric Eggly/PointSeven photo)

» TOM OVEREYNDER:
Not many 34 Big Jack
pocketknives are assembled with
PSF-27 blades and 18k-rose gold
pins and shield on jigged bone
handle scales.
(SharpByCoop photo)

« BEN KABISCH:
A classic spay blade trapper is
fashioned in a CPM 154 blade,
stainless bolsters and liners, and
stag handle scales.
(SharpByCoop photo)

» WANDER PAIM:
The "Gropius Balisong" gets around in a Sandvik stainless blade, ivory G-10 handle scales, and a titanium frame.

(SharpByCoop photo)

⌃ ENRIQUE PENA:
The classically styled Lanny's Clip front flipper sports a CPM 154 stainless blade, natural Micarta bolsters, and burlap Micarta handle scales.

(BladeGallery.com photo)

⌃ BOBBY HOUSE:
Antique stag handle scales and a Polish cross give the CPM 154 folder a classic look and feel.

(Eric Eggly/PointSeven photo)

» JIM DUNLAP:
Stag handle slabs with a Remington bullet shield highlight the two-blade CPM 154 flush-joint folder.

(Mitchell D. Cohen Photography)

« GRANT and GAVIN HAWK:
An out-the-front automatic "Deadlock Model C" folder comes in a CPM 20V blade, and a titanium frame engraved by Jake Newell.
(Mitchell D. Cohen Photography)

« W.D. PEASE:
The saddle horn trappers enlist Robert Eggerling mosaic damascus bolsters, CPM 154 blades, and mammoth ivory and sheep horn handles.
(Eric Eggly/PointSeven photo)

» EVAN NICOLAIDES:
The "Longhorn prototype" takes advantage of CPM 20CV steel, and checkered Westinghouse ivory paper Micarta.
(Mitchell D. Cohen Photography)

« LUKE SWENSON:
Fashioning a four-blade CPM 154 congress with integral liners and bolsters, dressed in stag, is akin to manufacturing a Lamborghini.
(SharpByCoop photo)

Fashionable Flippers

⌃ CORY MARTIN:
The contrast between the mirror-polished blade, zirconium bolsters, and the combination of Lightning Strike carbon fiber and vintage butterscotch Micarta handle scales is one we won't be forgetting soon.
(Mitchell D. Cohen Photography)

⌃ HERUCUS BLOMERUS:
Break out the mammoth ivory-handle flipper with Vinland Damasteel guard and Loki-pattern bolsters. Boo-yah!
(SharpByCoop photo)

⌃ RAFAL BRZESKI:
A green/black ZircuTi handle gives the "Gava" flipper folder with Bohler M390 blade a look all its own.
(Eric Eggly/PointSeven photo)

⌃RIAAN MANSER:

Crosscut "White Storm" FatCarbon handle inlays in black G-10 set the Bohler M390 flipper folder on fire.

(BladeGallery.com photo)

⌃IAN TYSON-PICKARSKI:

The "Elkin" LinerLock folder showcases a "Tiffany Blue" NTPT (North Thin Ply Technology) laminated composite handle, dark titanium accents, bronze "Zirblast" liners, and a ghost flipper tab.

(Mitchell D. Cohen Photography)

⌃A2—ANDRE THORBURN and ANDRE VAN HEERDEN:

The M390 stainless tanto blade of the flipper folder runs off a ceramic IKBS (Ikoma Korth Bearing System) and is accompanied by a black G-10 handle frame with dyed and stabilized oak burl inlays.

(BladeGallery.com photo)

⌃PETER CAREY:

The Stinger titanium frame-lock folder penetrates via a CPM S35VN blade.

(Mitchell D. Cohen Photography)

» TONY SEVERIO:
The full spectrum of a "Swamp Clipper" frame-lock flipper folder involves a 300-layer feather damascus blade and a heat-colored titanium handle frame with stainless hardware.

(Jocelyn Frasier photo)

» JOHN ARNOLD:
The precision of the M390 powdered metallurgical stainless blade only adds to the appeal of a front flipper with black G-10 handle frame and wild olive burl inlays.

(BladeGallery.com photo)

» PAUL KILBY:
Exhibiting obvious fashion sense, the maker equipped the bird-and-trout-style flipper folder with an Alabama Damascus blade, Fordite (years of layered paint from an old auto plant paint room) handle scales, and a titanium frame and liners.

(Mitchell D. Cohen Photography)

» FRANCOIS DU TOIT:
A Gold Dark Matter FatCarbon handle and stainless damascus bolsters lend character to an RWL-34 flipper folder.

(BladeGallery.com photo)

《 NATI AMOR:
Watch out—the Grosserosen
Damacore blade of the Whiplash flipper
might snap back at you if you don't
hold the titanium and mammoth ivory
handle tightly.
(Mitchell D. Cohen Photography)

《 HELGARD and IDA MOSTERT:
An engraved Celtic cross (Ida) is
the centerpiece of a stainless
flipper folder with carbon-
fiber handle scales.
(BladeGallery.com photo)

《 MICHAEL BURCH:
A Damasteel "Micro Boson" inset-
lock flipper folder incorporates a
Damasteel blade, carbon-fiber inlays,
and Westinghouse Micarta collars and
backspring.
(Mitchell D. Cohen Photography)

》 ENRIQUE PENA:
The "Raptor" front flipper
marries a CPM 154 blade
with Timascus bolsters and
green Micarta handle scales.
(BladeGallery.com photo)

» LOURENS PRINSLOO:
This fabulous little flipper folder sports a 2.75-inch Elmax stainless blade, a gold Dark Matter FatCarbon handle, and an IKBS (Ikoma Korth Bearing System) pivot.

(BladeGallery.com photo) photo)

» STEVEN SKIFF JR. and SR.:
Grooved and gorgeous, the "Culprit" frame-lock flipper features a Damasteel blade, titanium handle, and zirconium accents.

(SharpByCoop photo)

» ERIC LUTHER:
Grooved and groovy titanium and CPM 154 make up the Luck model.

(Mitchell D. Cohen Photography)

⌃ KEN ONION:
The slim CPM 154 "Rune" flipper is equipped with a textured and anodized titanium frame in bronze and golden hues.

(Mitchell D. Cohen Photography)

« PETER MARTIN:
"Grizz" gets the multi-bar Turkish twist damascus blade treatment, as well as "blacked out" superconductor bolsters, and sambar stag handle scales.
(Cory Martin photo)

⤴ KIRK MAYBERRY:
The Fatboy flipper has an acid-washed CPM 154 blade, zirconium bolsters, and red CarboQuartz handle scales.
(Mitchell D. Cohen Photography)

⤴ FRANCOIS MASSYN:
The carbon-fiber handle scales of a Bohler N690 flipper folder are inlaid with Lava Flow FatCarbon bolsters.
(BladeGallery.com photo)

⤴ LEE LERMAN:
A mirror-polished "Sigma 6" RWL-34 frame-lock folder features satin-finished flats, a titanium frame and hardware, and a blued meteorite backspacer and pivot inlays.
(Mitchell D. Cohen Photography)

Crème de la Crème Chef's Knives

» JEFF SWANSON:
A petite Gyuto enlists a 5.33-inch san mai blade with a V-Toku 2 carbon steel core, a Macassar ebony handle, and buffalo horn bolster.
(BladeGallery.com photo)

» DUSTIN DRIVER:
The combination of a Damasteel blade, carbon-fiber bolster, and Raffir wood handle is a sweet stew, indeed.
(SharpByCoop photo)

« AARON WILBURN:
The satin-finished 52100 blade and stabilized amboyna burl handle scales set on a full tang will do the job in the kitchen.
(BladeGallery.com photo)

« SCOTT FOX:
The shape and textured flats of the 52100 chef's knife set it apart, as do the dyed box elder burl and curly maple handle, and brass spacer and pin.
(Jocelyn Frasier photo)

《 MERT TANSU:
Stirring the pot is a
9.5-inch Wootz crucible
steel chef's knife that
includes a mammoth
ivory handle and a
bronze bolster.

(Caleb Royer photo)

《 MARK CORDINA:
The K-tip Gyuto comes in a
"Spicy White" san mai blade,
stabilized big leaf maple handle,
and stabilized ebony bolster.

(Rod Hoare photo)

》 EDUARDO BERARDO:
Handwork includes
a forged ladder-pattern
damascus blade and sculpted
stabilized maple burl handle.

(BladeGallery.com photo)

《 JESSE WANG:
A smoky hamon (temper line) wafts along
the length of a W2 blade on a chef's knife
that also sports a desert ironwood grip,
G-10 bolster, and bronze spacer.

(SharpByCoop photo)

« ED SOL:
This sweet chef's knife is realized in 52100 steel and a resin handle by Voodoo Resins.
(Mitchell D. Cohen Photography)

« BRANDON HAMPTON:
There's nothing raw or even undercooked about the wood-handle sushi chef's knife.
(Mitchell D. Cohen Photography)

« TOM BUCKNER:
The maker stirs the pot via a Damasteel twist-pattern damascus chef's knife in an exhibition-grade curly Koa handle.
(BladeGallery.com photo)

» JAMES BISHOP:
The black damascus blade and buffalo horn handle of the Gyuto are set off by a "Mexican Blanket" Micarta bolster.
(Rod Hoare photo)

» BRENT STUBBLEFIELD:
Key ingredients of a 9-inch integral chef's knife include multi-bar damascus, maple burl, and Micarta.

(Caleb Royer photo)

» JASON KNIGHT:
When you have an integral damascus chef's knife with Koa wood handle, there's no dish you can't make.

(SharpByCoop photo)

» KYLE DAILY:
This S-ground crème de la crème chef's knife sports a stabilized old-growth oak burl handle and "blocks" file work on the spine.

(Cory Martin photo)

« CH'IEN TURNER:
Truly a treat, the damascus chef's knife is garnished with a red/orange dyed curly maple handle, and a brass bolster.

(BladeGallery.com photo)

« CHARLIE ELLIS:
An integral damascus chef's knife features a highly figured, stabilized, and spalted hackberry handle.
(BladeGallery.com photo)

« LEO POTTER:
Stabilized spalted silkwood pinned on a canvas Micarta frame sets off a hand-forged 1084 chef's knife.
(BladeGallery.com photo)

» JAYDEN SIMISKY:
Say "mosaic damascus keyhole integral chef's knife" 10 times real fast. This feather-light example showcases a stabilized box elder burl handle.

» MARK SINCLAIR:
The kitchen petty is accomplished via a full flat-ground san mai blade, stabilized sassafras handle, mosaic pins, and G-10 liners.
(Rod Hoare photo)

《 CHRIS BERRY:
It turns out a toxic/aqua/jade marbled G-10 handle is the perfect choice for a chef's knife with a CPM MagnaCut steel blade.

(Mitchell D. Cohen Photography)

《 RICHARD PATTERSON:
A clean chef's knife is done up in a 52100 blade, and a dyed and stabilized maple burl grip.

(SharpByCoop photo)

》 WILLIAM KALKBRENNER:
If looking for a sweet Laotian rosewood-handle, integral chef's knife with forged W2 blade, you've come to the right place.

(BladeGallery.com photo)

《 DAN TOMPKINS:
The octagonal handle of a damascus chef's knife is Tasmanian blackwood butted up against an ancient bog oak spacer.

(SharpByCoop photo)

» SAM REED:
The nicely shaped 7.5-inch chef's knife sports a hand-forged 52100 blade and an Arizona desert ironwood handle.
(BladeGallery.com photo)

» GEOFFREY BAZE:
The straightforward ingredients of a 9-inch chef's knife are high-carbon steel and Tasmanian blackwood.
(SharpByCoop photo)

« JOSE SANTIAGO-CUMMINGS:
The Nitro-V stainless Nakiri vegetable chopper features a buffalo horn bolster with fine silver dot inlays, composite stone and black and yellow spacers, a dyed maple handle, and mahogany butt cap.
(Caleb Royer photo)

« MARTIN MOENNING:
The "Bluebell Chef's Knife" integrates an A2 tool steel blade, and a blue Ritchlite handle with a mosaic pin.
(Cory Martin photo)

》 SCOTT SWEDER:
A mammoth ivory spacer breaks up the blackness of a damascus blade and African blackwood handle.
(Mitchell D. Cohen Photography)

《 BEN AKIN:
Enter the AEB-L stainless chef's knife in a hand-rubbed finish, curly Koa handle, and mosaic and nickel silver pins.
(Jocelyn Frasier photo)

《 MICHAEL LANDSIEDEL:
Just guessing that most moms' paring knives weren't damascus models with brass guards and curly maple handles.
(SharpByCoop photo)

《 ANDREW MEERS:
No mere storebought chef's knife, the integral S-ground Gyuto boasts an 80CrV2 blade, black palm handle, and engraved bolsters in a basil leaf theme.
(BladeGallery.com photo)

» ARYEH GOLDENSON:
The chef's knife is a blend
of Vegas Forge "Fireball"
damascus, G-10 bolsters,
and Micarta handle scales.
(Mitchell D. Cohen Photography)

» MARK MOSTERT:
Get a load of that Cu-Mai blade
with copper and carbon steels,
as well as the dyed and stabilized
masur birch handle of the K-Tip
Gyuto chef's knife.
(BladeGallery.com photo)

⌃ DERRICK WULF:
A sleek chef's knife sports
a stabilized amboyna burl
handle, a carbon-fiber
and titanium bolster, and
a 1.2419 carbon tungsten
steel blade.
(Mitchell D. Cohen Photography)

» ISAIAH SCHROEDER:
The Gyuto in a dramatic
damascus blade, fine silver
bolster, and African blackwood
handle could be your go-to
chef's knife.
(SharpByCoop photo)

» MATTHEW PARKINSON:
A floral motif highlights the maple handle and AEB-L blade of a 7-inch chef's knife.
(SharpByCoop photo)

« JORDON BERTHELOT:
In the 6-inch chef's knife category comes a Baker Forge and Tool "Tiger-mai" damascus piece with a two-color mokume-gane bolster, and an ancient walrus ivory handle.
(Caleb Royer photo)

« THOMAS FRANKLIN:
A 54-layer crushed-ladder-pattern damascus blade is anchored by a D-shaped Koa handle and a G-10 collar. And it does crush it.
(Caleb Royer photo)

« C. LUIS PINA:
Stabilized spalted maple and damascus are the key ingredients of an exquisite integral chef's knife.
(BladeGallery.com photo)

Money Micarta

I would have chosen wooly mammoth tooth or tusk, Timascus, verdite or olivine, curly maple, or lightning strike carbon fiber. If someone were to have asked me what knife handle material I thought would be the most surprising, beautiful, lasting and innovatively employed in 2023 and '24, Micarta would not have been my answer.

With all the epoxies, phenolics, acrylics and polymers out there, the resin-infused woods, MokuTi and mokume-gane, Thunderstorm Kevlar, CarboQuartz, meteorite, C-Tech, Richlite and Kirinite, among a myriad of other handle materials, Micarta being the odds-on favorite for knife handles would have seemed a long shot to me. That's why I don't play the stock market.

I mean, really, check out the colorful array of Micarta herein, how it's used, combined with other materials, manipulated, and made into gorgeous knives, and then tell me it's not on the money.

Just when you think streaming music has taken over the record industry, people start buying turntables and .33 albums again. I'd say Micarta is making a comeback, but it never really went away. Like Westinghouse itself, it's here to stay. Money Micarta is where I'm hedging my bets from now on, and I'm feeling safe.

« EDDIE RAY:
The CPM 154 game skinner showcases an experimental black linen Westinghouse Micarta handle with a canvas Micarta overlay.
(Mitchell D. Cohen Photography)

« NICK TIMPSON:
The combination of G-10 and Micarta, with stainless chevrons in between, now that's the way to handle a CPM 154 folder (fashioned for the maker's wife).
(SharpByCoop photo)

« ENRIQUE PENA:
Denim Micarta makes a statement on the "Cabarello" front flipper with Timascus bolsters and a CPM 154 stainless blade.
(BladeGallery.com photo)

» NEAL GREEN:
The contrast between the pebble-finished MagnaCut blade, green Micarta handle, and red G-10 spacers is money.
(Jocelyn Frasier photo)

« JOSH MORGAN:
The claw-like "Twisted W's" damascus blade is secured via CopperMascus bolsters and a canvas Micarta grip.
(Eric Eggly/PointSeven photo)

» JESS HOFFMAN:
The 12C27 stainless "Roscommon" full-tang fixed blade dons cross-cut Westinghouse canvas Micarta handle scales with black spacers underneath.
(Cory Martin photo)

« A2—ANDRE THORBURN and ANDRE VAN HEERDEN:
A premium Damasteel stainless damascus flipper folder showcases Timascus bolsters and antique Westinghouse Micarta handle scales.
(BladeGallery.com photo)

≪ JASON RITCHIE:
A Tony Bose-pattern trapper showcases CPM 154 blades, stainless bolsters, and vintage Westinghouse linen Micarta handle scales.

(Cory Martin photo)

≪ MYKEL PIPER:
Money Micarta in this case involves a coin (shown for scale) and a natural canvas Micarta-handle micro Kiridashi with a chisel-ground CPM S45VN blade.

(SharpByCoop photo)

≪ PETER CAREY:
Westinghouse Micarta handles are combined with Mike Sakmar mokume-gane for the handle of the Cornerstone Mini Prototype in a Mike Norris "Fireclone 2" damascus blade.

(Mitchell D. Cohen Photography)

≫ BRIAN BROWN:
The honey and cream of the Falke V2S folder with Mike Norris Turkish Twist damascus blade are vintage orange paper Micarta and Westinghouse Ivorite.

(SharpByCoop photo)

≋ DON HANSON III:
A slimline trapper features a W2 blade, Westinghouse Micarta handle, and a stainless shield and pins.

(SharpByCoop photo)

» MATTHEW CHRISTENSEN:
The whole "Dreadeye" package includes a Chad Nichols Boomerang Armor-core san mai blade, Timascus bolsters, spacer, clip, and thumb studs, and Westinghouse Micarta handle scales.

(Mitchell D. Cohen Photography)

» JEREMY MARSH:
The Damasteel LinerLock gets the full black CarboQuartz, red G-10, and Westinghouse Micarta handle treatment.

(Mitchell D. Cohen Photography)

« MIKE MACINNES:
Blue G-10 bookends the stag handle and Micarta spacer of a forged 5160 hunter.

(Cory Martin photo)

» TONY BAKER:
If the green-dyed burlap Micarta feels as good in the hand as it looks in the eye, the PSF-27 drop-point hunter is one hot commodity.

(BladeGallery.com photo)

« PAT BIGGIN:
The stonewashed 80CrV2 blade goes perfectly with the dimpled black Micarta handle.

(Cory Martin photo)

《 DEON NEL:
Done up correctly with green canvas Micarta handle scales, the Bob Loveless-style chute knife also enlists a hollow-ground, mirror-polished N690 stainless blade.

(BladeGallery.com photo)

》 BRANDON CORBINL:
The Jab model showcases Chad Nichols' "Intrepid Core" damascus, Fat Carbon bolsters, butterscotch Westinghouse Micarta handle scales, and a black lip mother-of-pearl inlay in the back spacer.

(Mitchell D. Cohen Photography)

》 TREVOR BURGER:
Natural Micarta butts up beautifully against the bead-blasted titanium bolsters of an M390 stainless front flipper folder.

(BladeGallery.com photo)

《 BRIAN EFROS:
Green canvas Micarta tastefully contrasts with the Chad Nichols' "Roundabout" damascus blade.

(Mitchell D. Cohen Photography)

» JOSHUA FISHER:
The hand-forged W2 vegetable cleaver shows off a cloudy temper line and a vintage Micarta grip set on a full tang.
(BladeGallery.com photo)

« DAVID JESSIE II:
Multi-color Micarta proved a masterful handle choice for the "Lil' Britches" CPM 154 fixed blade.
(Mitchell D. Cohen Photography)

» TOMMY GANN:
Set turquoise in black Micarta, and it's going to pop on a ladder-pattern damascus EDC utility knife.
(BladeGallery.com photo)

« PAUL KILBY:
Vintage end-cut Micarta is the perfect counterpart to superconductor bolsters and a Damasteel blade.
(Mitchell D. Cohen Photography)

⌃ JENSEN BERGMAN:
The "Uncle Charlie" frame-lock folder attends the family reunion in a compound chisel-ground ladder-pattern damascus blade and an antique Westinghouse ivory Micarta handle with a CarboTi underlay.

(Mitchell D. Cohen Photography)

⌃ EVAN NICOLAIDES:
Checkered butterscotch Micarta dresses up the CPM 20CV "Barracuda" slip-joint folder.

(Mitchell D. Cohen Photography)

» CRAIG BROSMAN:
The money shot of a Bob Loveless-style hunter might be the canvas Micarta grip, but the CPM 154 blade with tapered tang and the red G-10 liners deserve recognition.

(Mitchell D. Cohen Photography)

⌃ CLIFF PARKER:
Antique rag Micarta is brought back to life for the handle of a W2 slip-joint folder with Art Deco mosaic damascus bolsters.

(BladeGallery.com photo)

» WILL STELTER:
Emerald-green paper Micarta is the "money" handle material of choice for a mosaic damascus fixed blade that is 4.75 inches overall.
(SharpByCoop photo)

⌃ BRYAN MONTALVO:
Resulting in a version of red, white and blue, the Alpha Pup locking-liner folder sports ivory Westinghouse Micarta handle scales with Bakelite spacers. The Vegas Forge blade is a beauty.
(Mitchell D. Cohen Photography)

« RICK NOWLAND:
Burlap Micarta makes a showing on a CPM 154 trapper with integral stainless bolsters and liners.
(BladeGallery.com photo)

» EDDIE STALCUP:
Black paper Micarta envelops the crosscut mammoth ivory handle scales of a CPM 154 hunter.
(SharpByCoop photo)

» JAMES BUCKLEY:
Westinghouse paper Micarta handle scales pop off a harpoon folder in a stonewashed CPM S30V blade.
(Mitchell D. Cohen Photography)

Clinch Pick, Utility & EDC Knives

A clinch pick has been precisely defined as a fixed-blade utility knife with an overall length of 5.5 inches and a 2 5/8-inch, single, reverse edge that is sharpened on the spine of the blade, not the belly. Largely used for self-defense, other applications of the clinch pick include everyday carry (EDC) and utility. The design purportedly also makes for an amazing box cutter and letter opener.

Other utility and EDC knives, sharpened on the bellies of the blades, or not having reverse edges or sharp spines, have borrowed design elements from clinch picks, including what are often rounded or bulbous handles, and similar blade and handle lengths and styles.

Could we have a new category in knives, or is this just an expansion of the increasingly popular EDC segment? The market will tell, but one thing is for sure, knifemakers are having fun fashioning clinch pick, utility, and EDC knives for eager users and collectors. Let the clinch pick cutting commence!

« COLLIN MAGUIRE:
Equally suitable for self-defense, everyday carry, and utility, the clinch pick model showcases a two-bar Firestorm damascus blade, a mastodon ivory handle, and black G-10 liners.
(SharpByCoop photo)

« JIM POLING:
The maker calls his everyday carry knives "BPK's" (Basic Poling Knives), these of the 1075 steel and Movingui (Nigerian satinwood) variety.
(SharpByCoop photo)

» RYAN SCHWARTZ:
The "Warble" fixed blade sports a W2 blade with wavy temper line, and red stag handle scales.

(Mitchell D. Cohen Photography)

« BOB RANKIN:
What doesn't this pocket EDC knife have going on? Start with an old bullet forged into the damascus blade, progress to the Fordite (layered automotive paint) bolsters, and end at the bog oak handle scales.

(SharpByCoop photo)

« MARCUS LIN:
Referring to the knife as a "miniature sharpened pry bar," the maker gave it a Takefu san mai blade with a VG-10 core, and a black canvas Micarta handle secured using brass tubing rivets.

(SharpByCoop photo)

STATE OF THE ART

You don't draw in the steel. The steel draws you in. You don't draw it back. It draws you back. When forging knife blades, the steel lets you know when the ore is heated to the core, and it's time to pound off slag and get the billet right back into the burning forge. The steel lets the bladesmith know when it's time to keep forging or draw back the temperature. The smith studies the steel and understands when it's time to draw the steel back, and when it should be quenched and cooled. The steel lets the smith know.

The author doesn't compose the book. The book composes itself. The author doesn't determine "State of the Art" categories. The categories determine themselves and are revealed to the author. The knifemakers create the categories. The author's job is to recognize them and include the best of the best in the book. He is only the interpreter, translator, medium and go-between.

Forged feather-damascus blades have been a hot category for a few years, and the bladesmiths have evolved the patterns and reinterpreted them. They still splay out, but in different directions and with light touches. Woodworkers are using dyes to catch the eyes and adding resins to the mix. Sculptors are sculping, scrimshanders scrimming, engravers engraving and carvers carving.

Bladesmiths are creating new and innovative mosaic patterns, forging copper into the blades themselves, elongating and enlivening ladder patterns, and of course forging san mai or "Clad-to-the-Core" steel patterns. The damascus cuts deep, and the many of the knifemakers still have "Golden Touches." Enjoy the "State of the Art" section. It's a living, breathing entity, and a creation all its own.

Decorated Daggers

» MATTHEW PARKINSON:
An L6 art dagger looks dashing in its sculpted tin-and-bronze guard and pommel, and fluted birch handle.
(SharpByCoop photo)

« JOHN DAVIS:
The California dagger parades a "Silver Streak" damascus blade, walrus ivory handle, and a silver sheath engraved by Dale Bass.
(Eric Eggly/PointSeven photo)

« JAMES EMMONS:
Standing tall is a ladder-pattern damascus dagger in a silver wire-inlaid, fluted blackwood handle, and a stainless guard and pommel.
(Jocelyn Frasier photo)

» MARK MOSTERT:
A skillfully fashioned mosaic damascus dagger benefits from bronze fittings and a stabilized buckeye burl handle.
(BladeGallery.com photo)

« ANDREW MEERS:
With a wavy blade like an Indonesian keris, the dynamic dagger is done up in damascus and stainless steel, including panda engraving and panda paw prints in 24-karat gold.
(SharpByCoop photo)

» STEPHEN VANDERKOLFF:
The maker said, "I think I'll fashion a Brad Millman damascus dagger with an agatized dinosaur bone handle," and so he did.
(Caleb Royer photo)

» KELLY VERMEER-VELLA:
A frame-handle takedown dagger is sent to market in a 1075-and-15N20-damascus blade and a mammoth ivory grip.

(Eric Eggly/PointSeven photo)

» DAVID BROADWELL:
An art deco dirk is created in a night (one side of the handle) and day (opposite side) theme, and includes a Chad Nichols stainless damascus blade, and a bronze guard and frame.

(SharpByCoop photo)

» DAVID LISCH:
"Mystic River" mosaic damascus helps the dagger flow from its tip to the faceted mosaic damascus guard, domed gold spacer, and carved blackwood handle with gold pins.

(SharpByCoop photo)

« JAMES BISHOP:
The "Death Watch Dagger" parades a twist-damascus blade and guard, and a damascus-pattern G-10 handle frame.

(Rod Hoare photo)

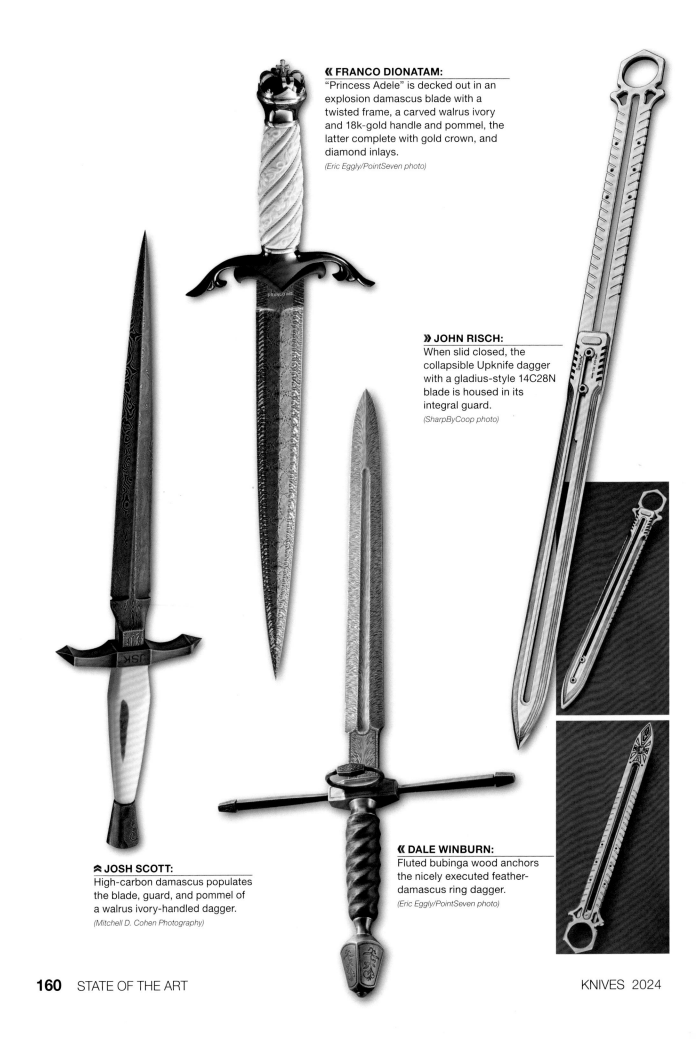

« FRANCO DIONATAM:
"Princess Adele" is decked out in an explosion damascus blade with a twisted frame, a carved walrus ivory and 18k-gold handle and pommel, the latter complete with gold crown, and diamond inlays.
(Eric Eggly/PointSeven photo)

» JOHN RISCH:
When slid closed, the collapsible Upknife dagger with a gladius-style 14C28N blade is housed in its integral guard.
(SharpByCoop photo)

⌃ JOSH SCOTT:
High-carbon damascus populates the blade, guard, and pommel of a walrus ivory-handled dagger.
(Mitchell D. Cohen Photography)

« DALE WINBURN:
Fluted bubinga wood anchors the nicely executed feather-damascus ring dagger.
(Eric Eggly/PointSeven photo)

《 MARDI MESHEJIAN:
The integral damascus push dagger is decorated with an anodized copper handle insert in a clover motif.

(SharpByCoop photo)

《 TOM OVEREYNDER:
The "Artemis Dagger" is a goddess alright, adorned in Hakkapella Damasteel, jade, diamonds, and Brian Hochstrat high-relief engraving with gold and platinum inlays.

(SharpByCoop photo)

》 EDMUND DAVIDSON:
If Mini Death Star daggers are your thing, and why wouldn't they be?, then you could do worse than the integral CPM 154 model in cape buffalo horn and Jere Davidson engraving.

(SharpByCoop photo)

》 NEELS VAN DEN BERG:
Symmetrical lines and coordinated accent colors make for an impressive damascus dagger.

(SharpByCoop photo)

⌃ JON MOORE:
The slim damascus dagger is the beneficiary of an aged Osage handle fashioned from an antique fence post, and blackened steel fittings.

» J.J. SIMON:
The ring dagger is defined by an 11-inch "Crushed-Ws"-damascus blade, a bronze guard, and silver wire-inlaid, fluted blackwood handle.
(SharpByCoop photo)

« SALEM STRAUB:
The dynamic damascus fighter comes with a twisted wire handle and a Teton Leather Company sheath.
(SharpByCoop photo)

» BUBBA CROUCH:
Engraved by Alice Carter, the integral dagger includes a hollow-ground CPM 154 blade, and mammoth ivory handle scales. It comes with a Paul Long leather sheath.
(SharpByCoop photo)

» JAVIER VOGT:
A guard-release auto dagger looks dapper in Doug Ponzio Turkish lace damascus, a Lee Marutti random-pattern damascus guard, mammoth ivory handle scales, and gold inlays throughout.
(SharpByCoop photo)

» JUSTIN CHENAULT:
A mosaic damascus dagger is done up properly in a fluted walrus ivory handle with twisted-wire overlay.
(Mitchell D. Cohen Photography)

» PETER MARTIN:
The ICBM folding dagger parades an Elmax steel blade, and CNC-textured anodized titanium handle scales, as well as a titanium back bar and pocket clip.

(Cory Martin photo)

« TYLER TURNER:
The perfectly executed integral Damasteel ring dagger showcases amethysts set in silver bezels on a stainless handle insert.

(Mitchell D. Cohen Photography)

» DENNIS FRIEDLY:
The damascus dagger is engraved by Alice Carter and Gil Rudolph.

(Eric Eggly/PointSeven photo)

⌃ BOB EARHART:
Balancing out the clamshell guard and wire-inlaid, fluted Gabon ebony handle is a 10.75-inch, 300-layer, ladder-pattern damascus blade.

(SharpByCoop photo)

» BRUCE SCHUBERT:
Stainless damascus, mild steel, stacked leather, copper, and nickel silver make up the "pig sticker" dagger.
(Rod Hoare photo)

« ANDERS HEDLUND:
One of the maker's incredible split-blade daggers, each edge of the "Eternal Twins" knife folds into opposite sides of the stainless handle, itself gold inlaid and engraved with a checkered mother-of-pearl grip.
(SharpByCoop photo)

« CODY HOFSOMMER:
A mosaic damascus quillon dagger is delivered in a fluted black ash burl handle wrapped in twisted Argentium silver wire.
(Mitchell D. Cohen Photography)

Forged Feather Work

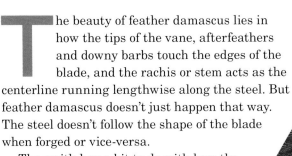

The beauty of feather damascus lies in how the tips of the vane, afterfeathers and downy barbs touch the edges of the blade, and the rachis or stem acts as the centerline running lengthwise along the steel. But feather damascus doesn't just happen that way. The steel doesn't follow the shape of the blade when forged or vice-versa.

The smith has a bit to do with how the patterns of steel and blade align. Combining skill, luck, and a bit of forging magic, oftentimes the bladesmith has a good idea of how the pattern will emerge from the steel while manipulating it, but not always, and rarely exactly. When forging steels together, they are heated, folded, and pounded, and after repeating the steps numerous times, the steel is crosscut and further forged until the maker can envision lines and patterns playing out.

The real pattern doesn't emerge until the billet is cut, ground, and finished, and the steel etched. The blade can be further manipulated and sharpened, but once finished, and etched, it's pretty much "forged feather work," and if that doesn't tickle your fancy then, it won't later either. It's a feather in the knifemaker's cap when the forged feather work floats like a butterfly and stings like a bee.

« MIKE DEIBERT:
If all feather damascus and African blackwood looked this good, there'd be no need for new knifemaking materials.
(SharpByCoop photo)

« BILL BEHNKE:
The maker refers to the blade as a "floral feather pattern" in O1, 15N20, and 1080 steels, and it's as bloomin' gorgeous as the stabilized feather crotch walnut handle.
(Cory Martin photo)

« TREVOR MORGAN:
Feather damascus is displayed on the blade of an integral chef's knife with stabilized eucalyptus handle.
(SharpByCoop photo)

⨾ FRANCOIS MAZIERES:
The drop-point hunter sports a Jim Poor feather-damascus blade, soldered bronze bolster, and Arizona desert ironwood handle.
(Rod Hoare photo)

» FRANK EDWARDS:
Gold dots on the feather damascus blade complement the hues of the bolsters and mammoth ivory handle scales.

(Eric Eggly/PointSeven photo)

« JEAN-PIERRE POTVIM:
The "Feather Fighter" is no featherweight, but instead a damascus and maple burl beast.

(SharpByCoop photo)

« MARK SINCLAIR:
Forged feather damascus and stabilized black Mulga wood make up the Gyuto chef's knife.

(Rod Hoare photo)

« ANDREW K. SMITH:
Let's assume a feather-damascus chef's knife with an amboyna burl handle is as light in the hand as it looks.

(SharpByCoop photo)

» BUBBA CROUCH:
The Mike Tyre feather damascus blades of a Tony Bose-style saddlehorn trapper float majestically above the red stag handle scales.

(SharpByCoop photo)

« JOHNNY STOUT:
Featuring a Bill Poor feather damascus blade and Joe Mason gold inlay and engraving, the "Compadre" also wears its mother-of-pearl handle inlay proudly.
(SharpByCoop photo)

« CHAD KENNEDY:
A fancy feather-damascus fighter showcases a silver wire-inlaid curly maple handle.
(SharpByCoop photo)

» SHAYNE CARTER:
The feather-damascus fighter is in fine form, handled here in stag.
(SharpByCoop photo)

» SCOTT SWEDER:
The maker's take on a feather damascus blade makes for a dramatic effect on a red mallee-handle fighter.
(SharpByCoop photo)

« TOBIN HILL:
Man, does that tail-lock folder look sweet in Mike Tyre feather damascus and mammoth ivory!
(SharpByCoop photo)

Sculpted Features

» EDWARD BURKE:
Sculpted bolsters befit the bone-handle switchblade with Matt Parkinson ladder-pattern-damascus blade.
(SharpByCoop photo)

« TOMMY CARROLL:
The Rose Sword and Rose Dagger are sculpted from 1095 steel and fitted with forged iron grips.
(Eric Eggly/PointSeven photo)

« BERTIE RIETVELD:
The maker sculpted the ladder-pattern damascus, meteorite, titanium, and lapis lazuli into a whopping, chopping, ultimately jaw-dropping "Griffin II."
(SharpByCoop photo)

« RON LAKE:
With Wolfgang Loerchner sculpting the stainless folders, good things happen when two masters come together.
(SharpByCoop photo)

» THEO NAZZ:
The tree in the handle of the "Library Kard" fixed blade is the frayed end of cable damascus forged for the blade.
(SharpByCoop photo)

» JOE SZILASKI:
Four buffalo heads are sculpted into the W2 pipe of a curly maple-hafted spike tomahawk that also features gold and silver inlays.
(SharpByCoop photo)

» JEAN-PIERRE POTVIM:
Check out the sculpted pommel and blade of the "El Violin de Vulcano" integral fixed blade in damascus and carved mammoth ivory.
(SharpByCoop photo)

» GUS CECCHINI:
It's a complete sculpture, from the tip of the blade to the butt of the handle and all points in between.
(SharpByCoop photo)

⌃ CORRADO MORO:
Oh, the gears in the knife keep on turnin', and the sculpted stainless handle and bolster area of the RWL-34 "Huayra" reveal it all.
(SharpByCoop photo)

Wood & Resin Fusion

If you've ever seen a wood-and-resin coffee table with what looks like a river of highly hued water, lava or molten steel running through the grains of the slabbed wooden top, then you understand the appeal of wood and resin fusion.

Knifemakers are inevitably at the lead of the artistic pack when it comes to trends and movements in the creative world. They might take their cues from other artists, but more often than not, bladesmiths and edged art makers are the innovative leaders, creating new materials, mechanisms and aesthetic concepts that elevate their craft to new heights.

Wood and resin fusion is just one way they put a spotlight on the knife industry and highlight the handcraft of blade making. So many embellishments and techniques enter the knife world that wood and resin fusion might seem like another passing trend, yet the argument can be made that the practice is here to stay. There are enough ways to play with the married materials to make them utilitarian and aesthetic, which is what sets knives apart from other art forms and distinguishes the craft in the first place.

« ANDY ISAACKS:
The handle scales of a mirror-polished CPM 154 drop-point hunter are a hybrid of Asian satinwood and green resin.
(Jocelyn Frasier photo)

« JOSE SANTIAGO-CUMMINGS:
An AEB-L stainless cook's knife features a brass-inlaid buffalo horn, composite turquoise, stabilized cherry wood, and blue resin handle.
(Jocelyn Frasier photo)

Copper Showstoppers

Whether they are five-steel GoMai blades, or you refer to them as Shichi mai damascus, Cu Mai, Cu Shim, or a myriad of other names, damascus clad with other alloys, in this case copper, is about as state of the art in the knife industry as it gets.

Copper lines run through the steel like calcite, quartz and other mineral veins through rock, the difference being that these aren't cavities or cracks in the steel where minerals have deposited. This is the forging of alloys together, the science of metallurgy at its finest, making patterns, taking steel to its core, and then giving it character, bringing it to life, breathing fire into its being, and polishing it to a sheen.

What's new in knives—copper showstoppers, that's what, and the finest smithies in the land are making sure there's enough material for knifemakers to pound out some of the prettiest blades this side of the Eastern Pampas grasslands. These are knives worth noting for their utilitarian use, state-of-the-art material makeup, and beauty to behold.

» ANDREW GRIGGS:
A copper-infused Baker Forge Shichi mai damascus blade is only one impressive part of the harpoon bowie, a second being the Ukrainian bog oak handle.
(SharpByCoop photo)

« DAN TOMPKINS:
A three-piece set of 4.5-inch hunters includes Baker Forge blades made up of 80CrV2 cores with copper liners, and bronze-and-15N20 damascus.
(Caleb Royer photo)

« GREYSON WELTYK:
A Baker Forge and Tool double damascus blade makes up one end of the hunting knife, the other being vintage linen Micarta bolsters, mammoth tusk handle slabs, and vintage pins and liners.
(Caleb Royer photo)

JIM HALLER:
In this case you want to hold a "Grudge"—the gorgeous knife with an Adam DeVille Cru Mai damascus blade, black linen Micarta handle scales, blue G-10 liners, and copper mosaic pins.

(Mitchell D. Cohen Photography)

DAN HUBBS:
The Cu Mai blade is accompanied by a copper-and-carbon-fiber composite handle, and a tooled and stamped leather sheath.

(SharpByCoop photo)

COREY HOLLEY:
A Baker Forge and Tool double damascus blade makes up one end of the hunting knife, the other being vintage linen Micarta bolsters, mammoth tusk handle slabs, and vintage pins and liners.

(Eric Eggly/PointSeven photo)

CHRIS FARRELL:
The wickedly ground Húrin model gets the full Baker Forge Cu Shim damascus GoMai blade treatment, along with a dyed, stabilized, and sculpted buckeye burl handle, and mosaic pin.

(SharpByCoop photo)

JAYDEN SIMISKY:
The copper, mild steel, and 1095 GoMai hunter/everyday carry knife is the beneficiary of a stabilized and dyed curly maple handle.

DAVID TUCKER:
The slip-joint trapper engages collectors via a Hitatchi Blue 2 Cu Mai blade, and a ringed Gidgee handle featuring Huon pine inlays over dual integral shields.

(Rod Hoare photo)

《 GERRY MICHAEL:
The makeup of the mindboggling blade is a 120-layer random damascus core, a layer of copper and 1095 steel, accompanied by a redwood burl handle, copper spacer, and marbled carbon-fiber bolster.
(Caleb Royer photo)

《 MARK MOSTERT:
Try not to stray far in following the lines of a hand-forged Cu-Mai blade on the chef's knife with an ironwood grip.
(BladeGallery.com photo)

《 MARK CORDINA:
The Cu Mai blade of the Gyuto chef's knife comes in an Aogami Super core forged together with copper, 1084, and mild steel, and is butted up against an African blackwood handle over a bronze and G-10 frame.
(Rod Hoare photo)

⌃ KELLY VERMEER-VELLA:
The beautiful Black Mamba bowie is brought to life in a copper and nickel Cuni-Mai damascus blade with a 1075 core, and an Afzelia Xylay burl handle.
(Eric Eggly/PointSeven photo)

⌃ MARCUS LIN:
The "Kahuna" is forged to shape by the maker in a Takefu Yu-Shoku steel blade that includes a high-carbon steel core with laminated sides of mokume-gane cladding—copper, brass, and stainless steel. The handle is a carbon-fiber core with a brass counterbalance at the rear.
(SharpByCoop photo)

Scrimshaw Sans Flaw

» HELGARD and IDA MOSTERT:
The ladder-pattern damascus front flipper showcases scrimshaw on imitation ivory and engraved titanium bolsters.

(BladeGallery.com photo)

« DANIELE IBBA:
Medusa Gorgona comes to life on a 440C integral art knife thanks to Roberto Bruci scrimshaw on white mother-of-pearl. Gemstone inlays include rubies, and green, yellow, and blue diamonds.

(SharpByCoop photo)

⌄ HERUCUS BLOMERUS:
Westinghouse paper Micarta is the medium of choice for bear scrimshaw on an HB-15 flipper folder.

(SharpByCoop photo)

« JIMMIE SMITH:
Scrimshaw in ivory on the CPM 154 clip-point fixed blade is of a water buffalo on one side of the handle, and a lion on the other, with bolsters engraved by Dale Bass to boot.

(SharpByCoop photo)

A Mosaic Matrix

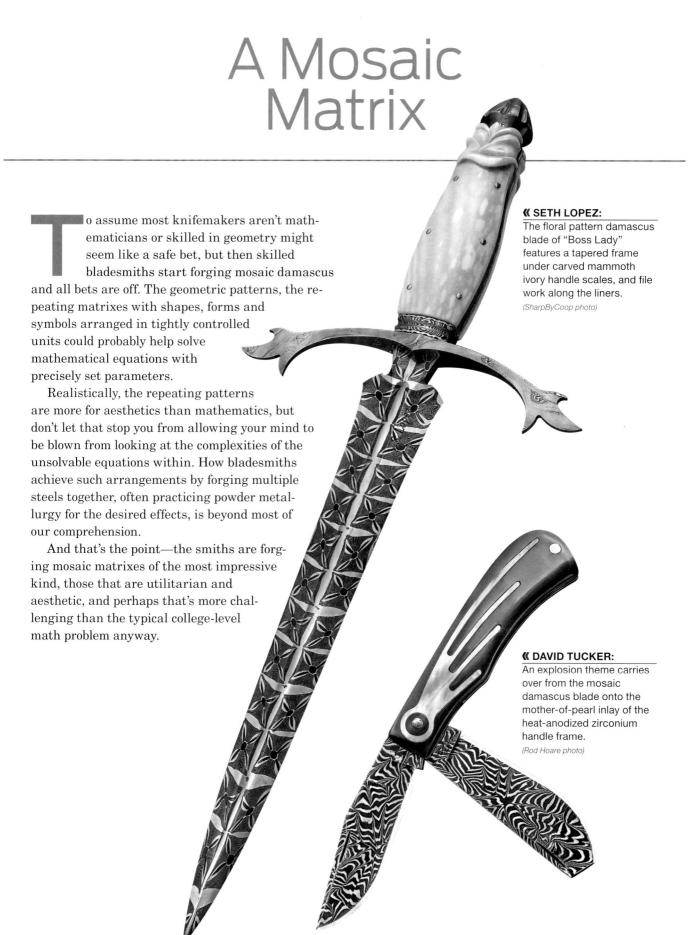

To assume most knifemakers aren't mathematicians or skilled in geometry might seem like a safe bet, but then skilled bladesmiths start forging mosaic damascus and all bets are off. The geometric patterns, the repeating matrixes with shapes, forms and symbols arranged in tightly controlled units could probably help solve mathematical equations with precisely set parameters.

Realistically, the repeating patterns are more for aesthetics than mathematics, but don't let that stop you from allowing your mind to be blown from looking at the complexities of the unsolvable equations within. How bladesmiths achieve such arrangements by forging multiple steels together, often practicing powder metallurgy for the desired effects, is beyond most of our comprehension.

And that's the point—the smiths are forging mosaic matrixes of the most impressive kind, those that are utilitarian and aesthetic, and perhaps that's more challenging than the typical college-level math problem anyway.

❮❮ SETH LOPEZ:
The floral pattern damascus blade of "Boss Lady" features a tapered frame under carved mammoth ivory handle scales, and file work along the liners.
(SharpByCoop photo)

❮❮ DAVID TUCKER:
An explosion theme carries over from the mosaic damascus blade onto the mother-of-pearl inlay of the heat-anodized zirconium handle frame.
(Rod Hoare photo)

» TANNER COUCH:
Amenities include a Bill Poor mosaic damascus blade, red stag handle, and arrowhead shield.
(Eric Eggly/PointSeven photo)

« JEFF ROYER:
A Western-style chef's knife boasts a beautiful mosaic damascus blade, a dyed and stabilized silkwood burl handle, and a custom copper guard.
(Jocelyn Frasier photo)

« ANDREW MEERS:
Once (if) you get past that mosaic damascus blade, behold the mild steel guard and pommel with an engraving inspired by rutilated quartz, and hibiscus engraving 24-karat gold.
(SharpByCoop photo)

« TOMMY GANN:
Mammoth ivory and mosaic damascus are beautiful bedfellows on an S-guard bowie with brass liners.
(Eric Eggly/PointSeven photo)

» ANDREW BLOMFIELD:
A sub-hilt ring guard bowie/fighter is adorned in a multi-bar mosaic damascus blade and one ringed Gidgee handle.
(BladeGallery.com photo)

» AUDRA DRAPER:
The maker's mosaic feather damascus blade is offset by a Rick Nowland mokume-gane guard and gold-lip mother-of-pearl handle.
(SharpByCoop photo)

« MARK BARRETT:
The mosaic damascus blade of the Gyuto chef's knife is properly paired with a Tasmanian blackwood handle, as well as brass and G-10 spacers.
(Rod Hoare photo)

« JUSTIN CHENAULT:
It's good to have mouthwatering mosaic damascus on a chef's knife, here in an amboyna burl handle, and blackened zirconium bolster.
(Mitchell D. Cohen Photography)

» SHAWN ELLIS:
An integral mosaic damascus field knife showcases ancient walrus ivory handle scales set with sterling silver pins.

(BladeGallery.com photo)

« DAVE SAUER:
The bowie benefits from amazing mosaic damascus pattern play, as well as a wrought iron guard and walrus tusk handle.

(SharpByCoop photo)

« JESSE HU:
The mesmerizing mosaic damascus K-tip has an S-ground blade, and a ringed Gidgee handle secured to a through-tang with a stainless pin.

(Caleb Royer photo)

« LOURENS PRINSLOO:
Forging mosaic damascus bolsters for an Elmax stainless flipper folder with green Dark Matter FatCarbon handle scales can't be a bad thing.

(BladeGallery.com photo)

» JIM MOENCK:
Mosaic damascus and mammoth ivory make for a fine pairing on the locking-liner folder, here with gold-plated screws.

(Mitchell D. Cohen Photography)

» MAX HARDER:
Look closely enough toward the heel of the mosaic damascus blade with twist damascus wrap, and one discerns the BLADE Show West logo 3-D printed in canister steel.

((SharpByCoop photo)

« CLIFF PARKER:
Via a mosaic damascus bolster rendering, the maker shows us where the giraffe bone handle scales originated.

(SharpByCoop photo)

» JARRETT CIESLAK:
A mosaic damascus fighter sports a wrought iron guard and sculpted curly maple handle.

(Mitchell D. Cohen Photography)

« JAYDEN SIMISKY:
So now they are 3D-printing mosaic damascus, here on a hunter with a stabilized box elder burl handle and brass pins.

⯆ PETER COCKS:
The "Desert Moth" mosaic damascus blade of the utility knife would take flight if not anchored by a red Morrell burl handle.
(Rod Hoare photo)

《 CLARENCE DEYONG:
Mosaic damascus makes a clip-point bowie come to life, that in a sambar stag handle with damascus guard and mosaic pommel.
(Mitchell D. Cohen Photography)

》 DAVID TUTHILL:
The mosaic damascus blade of the chef's knife will make mincemeat out of a roast and features an aptly named beefwood handle.
(BladeGallery.com photo)

《 RONNIE SMITH:
The fossil walrus ivory-handle mosaic damascus fighter dazzles its opponents before landing the knockout punch.
(Mitchell D. Cohen Photography)

» CHRIS SHARP:
Between the sharp barbs of the mosaic damascus and those in the handle inlay, the stag-handle slip-joint will help keep the cows corralled.
(SharpByCoop photo)

⌃ RYAN SIMON:
A fine stag-handle bowie gets the full mosaic damascus treatment.
(Rod Hoare photo)

» TIM HANCOCK:
The late, great maker's full-tang damascus bowie benefits from file-worked liners and stag handle scales.
(SharpByCoop photo)

« GARY RODEWALD:
A ladder-W's-pattern mosaic damascus blade gets things rolling on the "Bitterroot Bowie" with Arizona desert ironwood grip.
(BladeGallery.com photo)

« SCOTT GALLAGHER:
The mosaic damascus blade plays a dramatic role on a 15-inch bowie with a fossil walrus handle and firecracker damascus guard.

(Jocelyn Frasier photo)

« BRENT STUBBLEFIELD:
The tightly patterned mosaic damascus blade of a chef's knife contrasts nicely with the amber spacer and Hawaiian Koa handle.

(SharpByCoop photo)

« AARON WILBURN:
The mosaic damascus blade will no doubt elicit smiles in the kitchen while gripping the ringed Gidgee handle of the chef's knife.

(BladeGallery.com photo)

» MICHAEL ANDERSSON:
The five-bar mosaic damascus blade of the clamshell bowie is as mesmerizing as that mammoth ivory handle.

(BladeGallery.com photo)

⌃ D.R. (DAVID) DAVIS:
Bookending the pearl handle scales of a two-blade serpentine jackknife are mosaic damascus bolsters and flat-ground stainless damascus blades.

(Mitchell D. Cohen Photography)

« CODY HOFSOMMER:
Mosaic damascus elevates the hunting knife to display case status, here combined with an ancient walrus ivory handle, and bronze spacer and finial.
(Mitchell D. Cohen Photography)

« DAVID LISCH:
One walrus ivory-handle pirate bowie features a "Mystic Butterflies" mosaic damascus blade and a forged damascus pommel split down the middle and wrapped around the wrought iron penny guard.
(SharpByCoop photo)

» JEFFREY DRISCOLL:
The multi-bar mosaic damascus blade forged by Gregory Verizhnikov butts up against stag bolsters and an African blackwood handle.
(BladeGallery.com photo)

⌃ WILL STELTER:
"Explosion Weave" mosaic damascus leaves its aftereffects across the blade of a Koa-handle chef's knife.
(SharpByCoop photo)

All Great Engravings

» JOHNNY STOUT:
"Conquistador" is a double-action auto folder fitted with a Jim Poor "Heatbeat" damascus blade, engraved and gold-inlaid bolsters by Dale Bass, and fluted mammoth ivory handle scales.

(Caleb Royer photo)

» CHARLES GEDRAITIS:
The scale-release auto comes alive in a Mike Norris "Gala Skin" damascus blade, a stainless frame, and Jake Newell engraving.

(SharpByCoop photo)

« JODY MULLER:
The dress locking folder proves the perfect palette for the maker's gold inlay, engraving, and damascus forging skills.

(SharpByCoop photo)

⌃ HELGARD and IDA MOSTERT:
With titanium bolsters engraved in Celtic knots by Ida, the front flipper folder also sports a satin-finished stainless blade, and Copper Flake FatCarbon handle scales set on titanium liners.

(BladeGallery.com photo)

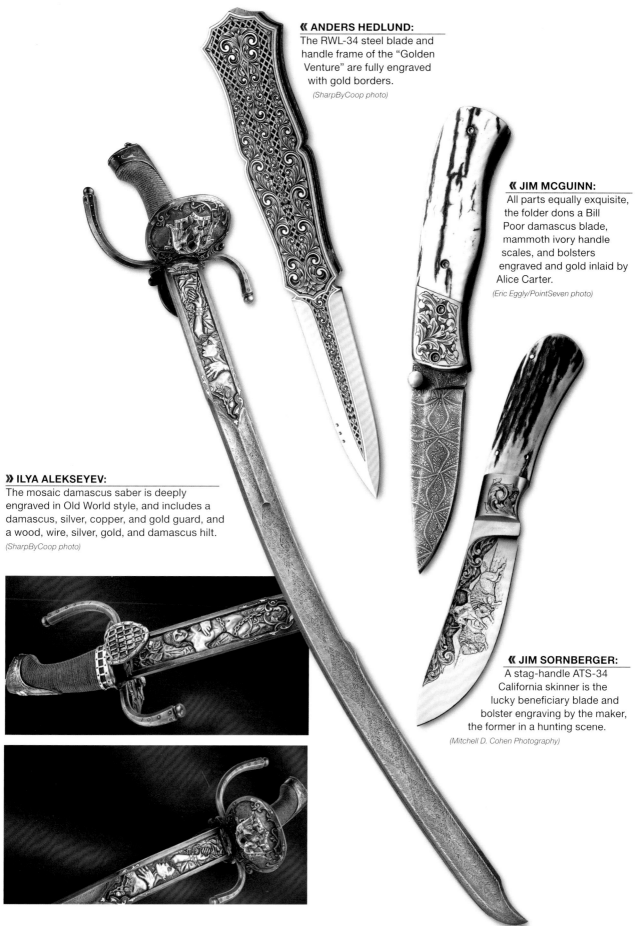

《 ANDERS HEDLUND:
The RWL-34 steel blade and handle frame of the "Golden Venture" are fully engraved with gold borders.
(SharpByCoop photo)

《 JIM MCGUINN:
All parts equally exquisite, the folder dons a Bill Poor damascus blade, mammoth ivory handle scales, and bolsters engraved and gold inlaid by Alice Carter.
(Eric Eggly/PointSeven photo)

》 ILYA ALEKSEYEV:
The mosaic damascus saber is deeply engraved in Old World style, and includes a damascus, silver, copper, and gold guard, and a wood, wire, silver, gold, and damascus hilt.
(SharpByCoop photo)

《 JIM SORNBERGER:
A stag-handle ATS-34 California skinner is the lucky beneficiary blade and bolster engraving by the maker, the former in a hunting scene.
(Mitchell D. Cohen Photography)

» JIM COFFEE:
Engraving by Chris Rossiter makes for a nice transition between the san mai blade and mammoth ivory handle scales.
(Mitchell D. Cohen Photography)

« ADAM RITCHIE:
A forest is beautifully etched on the chisel-ground O1 fixed blade that also features repurposed antique English knife handle scales.
(Mitchell D. Cohen Photography)

⌃ JEFF HAWKINS:
The Mike Tyre damascus blades and Alice Carter engraved bolsters highlight an amber stag-handle sowbelly.
(SharpByCoop photo)

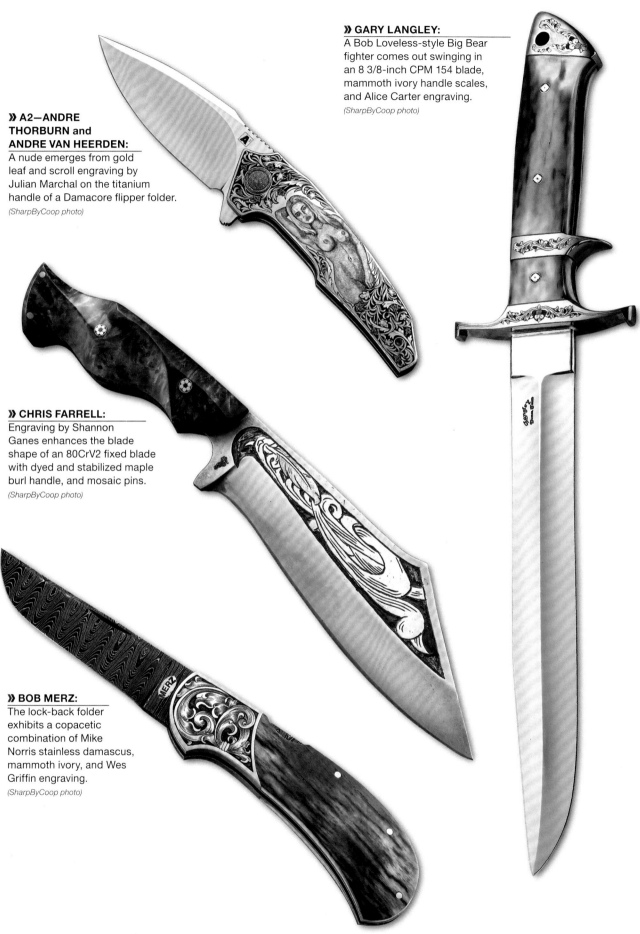

» GARY LANGLEY:
A Bob Loveless-style Big Bear fighter comes out swinging in an 8 3/8-inch CPM 154 blade, mammoth ivory handle scales, and Alice Carter engraving.
(SharpByCoop photo)

» A2—ANDRE THORBURN and ANDRE VAN HEERDEN:
A nude emerges from gold leaf and scroll engraving by Julian Marchal on the titanium handle of a Damacore flipper folder.
(SharpByCoop photo)

» CHRIS FARRELL:
Engraving by Shannon Ganes enhances the blade shape of an 80CrV2 fixed blade with dyed and stabilized maple burl handle, and mosaic pins.
(SharpByCoop photo)

» BOB MERZ:
The lock-back folder exhibits a copacetic combination of Mike Norris stainless damascus, mammoth ivory, and Wes Griffin engraving.
(SharpByCoop photo)

» FRANK EDWARDS:
The feather damascus blade seemingly splays out from the gold-inlaid and engraved bolsters of the front flipper folder with blue-green mammoth ivory handle scales.
(BladeGallery.com photo)

« EDMUND DAVIDSON:
Once you've perfected integral CPM 154 fixed blades, you add musk ox horn handles and ask Paul Markow to engrave them, and Paul Long to fashion sheaths for the artistic works.
(SharpByCoop photo)

⌃ JASON FRY:
Tasteful Alice Carter engraving adds highlights to the 81-layer damascus fixed blade with giraffe bone handle.
(Eric Eggly/PointSeven photo)

⌃ DENNIS FRIEDLY:
The CPM 154 hunter with mammoth ivory handle is part of a "Big Five" set engraved and gold inlaid by Gil Rudolph.
(SharpByCoop photo)

» TOM OVEREYNDER:
Engraving and gold inlay by Brian Hochstrat frame the black-lip pearl inlay of a Persian-style Damasteel gent's folder.
(SharpByCoop photo)

« MICHAEL ZIEBA:
The maker creates his vision of "per aspera ad astra" (through adversity to the stars) on the titanium handles of two Damasteel flipper folders.
(SharpByCoop photo)

« BUBBA CROUCH:
A mammoth ivory-handle CPM 154 trapper gets the full engraving treatment from Alice Carter, including the bolsters, spacer, blade, and handle shield.
(SharpByCoop photo)

« MICHAEL WALKER:
The Model 20 locking-liner folder shows a Slow Twist Damasteel blade and engraved handle.
(SharpByCoop photo)

» TOBIN HILL:
Sometimes one knows enough to have Alice Carter engrave and gold inlay a sodbuster lock-back folder with CPM-154 blade and red stag handle.

(SharpByCoop photo)

« VERONIQUE LAURENT:
The brass-framed, random-pattern damascus fixed blade parades a mother-of-pearl handle and engraved steel bolsters in a floral and butterfly motif.

(SharpByCoop photo)

« HERUCUS BLOMERUS:
Pretty pattern play on the flipper folder includes a Takefu SG2 damascus blade, and a ZircuTi handle engraved by Hendrik Viljoen.

(SharpByCoop photo)

« ANTON VAN DER WESTHUIZEN:
Masterful engraving by Julian Marchal on the titanium handle inlay and black Timascus frame depict a scene from the legendary tale of Queen Boudicca slaying a Roman soldier, all within the confines of a Damacore stainless damascus san mai flipper folder.

(BladeGallery.com photo)

» JIM POOR:
It took basketweave-pattern engraved front and rear bolsters to compete with the "Riptide" damascus blade of a slip-joint trapper.
(BladeGallery.com photo)

« TYLER TURNER:
The pearl-handle Damasteel toothpick model is all the better for the Jody Muller gold-inlay and engraving.
(SharpByCoop photo)

« SAMUEL LURQUIN:
The maker's Ural model sports some dizzying damascus, gorgeous wood grains, and stylish Elizabeth DaJusta engraving.
(SharpByCoop photo)

« STANLEY BUZEK:
With a River of Fire damascus blade and red stag handle scales, the trapper just called for Alice Carter bolster engraved.
(SharpByCoop photo)

Dyed in the Wood Practitioners

"Dyed in the wool" means holding strong opinions, uncompromising and unchanging or inveterate. One can be a dyed-in-the-wool sports fan, dyed-in-the-wool knife collector or dyed-in-the-wool hunter. Most knifemakers I know are definitely dyed-in-the-wool artisans. They have to be, or they'd never enter the field.

You can't be a halfhearted creative type, or you'll starve to death. One must be all in, and if not, then hold several jobs to support the knifemaking habit. Forging blades—dyed in the wool; engraving bolsters—dyed in the wool; scrimshawing knife handles—dyed in the wool; fashioning leather sheaths—dyed in the wool or die trying.

Then there are the dyed-in-the-wood practitioners. These guys and gals see beauty in burl, its grains, figuration and very pores. They shape, contour, and sand the wood, bringing out its inner beauty before staining and varnishing it. If they're really dedicated and want to give the wood their own signature flair, they'll dye it. Oh, dyed-in-the-wood practitioners are a special breed. They hold strong opinions, are uncompromising, unchanging, and inveterate.

« JOSE SANTIAGO-CUMMINGS:
A Nitro V stainless cook's knife with a dyed maple handle, composite stone bolster, and red liner is a colorful character.
(Caleb Royer photo)

« CHUCK COOK:
The 6-inch kitchen knife wears its stripes well—a dyed-blue and plain maple handle, as well as a 256-layer raindrop-damascus blade.
(SharpByCoop photo)

« CARL MICHAEL ALMQVIST:
With a multi-bar damascus blade forged by Konstantin Lysenko of Donetsk, Ukraine, the "Blue Dream" is named for its dyed and stabilized masur birch grip with damascus spacer.

(BladeGallery.com photo)

« BRETT SCHALLER:
Stabilized and dyed box elder burl brightens up a Bob Loveless-style sub-hilt fighter in CPM 154 steel.

(Jocelyn Frasier photo)

» JESS HOFFMAN:
The "Armagh" AEB-L paring knife gets it done in dyed buckeye burl.

(Cory Martin photo)

» FAYE LANKISTER:
Between the maker's own damascus and a dyed maple burl handle, the kitchen knife is something to savor.

(SharpByCoop photo)

» KELLY FRASIER: Stabilized and dyed birch burl anchors a 25C3 high carbon steel paring knife.

(SharpByCoop photo)

» DAN TOMPKINS: Features of a 10.5-inch chef's knife include a Baker Forge "Coppermascus" blade with an 80CrV2 core, a dyed and stabilized redwood handle, copper and G-10 spacers, and a G-10 bolster.

(Caleb Royer photo)

« DE WET VAN ZYL: Outstanding elements of a chef's knife are its san mai blade, copper guard, and dyed and stabilized curly maple handle.

(BladeGallery.com photo)

⌃ RIAAN MANSER: With a dyed and stabilized maple burl handle inlay framed out in black G-10, the Bohler M390 stainless front flipper folder is a looker.

(BladeGallery.com photo)

» JARRETT CIESLAK:
A 375-layer damascus belt knife sports a bronze guard, and a dyed and stabilized curly maple handle.
(BladeGallery.com photo)

» NOAH VACHON:
Spalted tamarind and buffalo horn provide the one-two punch for a 6-inch Nitro-V stainless utility chef's knife.
(Jocelyn Frasier photo)

« DERICK KEMPER:
Dyed box elder burl is a beautifying element on an already pretty twist-damascus bowie.
(SharpByCoop photo)

Clad-to-the-Core Steel

San mai or clad damascus steel has been around since at least the 14th century A.D., long used by Japanese bladesmiths who forged katanas for flexibility and sharpness. Soft steels sandwiching hard steel cores allow the blades to absorb shock or bend slightly without breaking, and without sacrificing cutting and slicing ability.

The lamination technique is reserved for blades that have symmetrical grinds, or those ground from both sides to expose the central edges. If stainless alloys are used for the outer layers, they add corrosion resistance even if the edge is high-carbon steel.

But modern bladesmiths aren't satisfied with simply building superior blades with stainless properties, they also want them to look the part, and have gotten incredibly creative with material makeup and pattern welding.

Clad to the core, the blades herein are some of the sweetest san mai blades on the planet, forged for sharpness, strength, and flexibility, and often aesthetically superior to their 14th-century counterparts.

» MICAH DUNN:
The chef's knife sports an "oh my" Go-Mai blade, a red mallee burl handle, and a spalted chestnut spacer.
(Jocelyn Frasier photo)

» PAUL KILBY:
The full-dress flipper enlists a Chad Nichols Armorcore san mai blade, twisted MokuTi handle scales, and a zirconium pocket clip.
(Mitchell D. Cohen Photography)

« DAVID BRENIERE:
The "Ipanema" folder fares well in a san mai damascus blade, mosaic damascus bolsters, and mammoth ivory handle scales.
(SharpByCoop photo)

» JORDON BERTHELOT:
No ordinary 8-inch chef's knife, it features an Adam Deville half-feather-damascus blade, carbon fiber bolster, and a highly figured cottonwood handle from Rob Harrison (@ robswildwood).
(Caleb Royer photo)

« ANDREW MOCHADO:
Handled in black ash burl with an ebony bolster and white G-10 spacer, the chef's knife showcases an NBC san mai blade.
(Eric Eggly/PointSeven photo)

» PEDRO GONZALEZ:
The five-layer, coffee-etched Go-Mai blade of a redwood-handle fighter consists of an 80CrV2 carbon steel core surrounded by 15N20 and a final layer of 80CrV2.

(BladeGallery.com photo)

« DAVID TUCKER:
An interframe slip-joint trapper is outfitted in a Damasteel "Hakkapella Damacore" blade, and a mill-relieved and jeweled Chad Nichols dark titanium handle frame with a black-lip-pearl inlay.

(Rod Hoare photo)

« CLARENCE DEYONG:
This hot little hunter is clad in a san mai blade, sambar stag handle scales, and mosaic pins.

(Mitchell D. Cohen Photography)

« ZHAO YUPENG:
The maker's artistic take on a push dagger includes a boomerang damascus blade with an XHP core, a zirconium guard, and wood handle scales.

(SharpByCoop photo)

≪ DONALD DULEVICH:
A stunning chef's knife parades a stainless damascus clad CuMai blade with a Nitro-V core by Gregg Dion, a Koa and maple burl handle, Trustone spacer, and copper and G-10 shims.
(Jocelyn Frasier photo)

≪ HENNIE DU PLESSIS:
The san mai blade of the folder has a VG-10 core and is accompanied by a mokume-gane bolster and desert ironwood handle scales.
(BladeGallery.com photo)

≫ WILLIE VAN DER MERWE
The Go-Mai blade of the bowie is forged from carbon steels with 24k-gold inlay, and married with a nickel silver guard, maple burl handle, and zirconium spacers.
(BladeGallery.com photo)

≫ MARCUS LIN:
An Americanized version of a Honesuke Maru with improved handle contours for retention, the maker forged the Takefu san mai damascus blade to shape and used black canvas Micarta for the grip.
(SharpByCoop photo)

❯ TONY CETANI:
Few paring knives are delivered in raindrop damascus blades over 80CrV2 cores, or spalted ash handles for that matter.
(Caleb Royer photo)

❯ ANDRE THORBURN:
A pristine flipper folder is outfitted in a san mai blade with an SG2 core, and a black G-10 handle frame featuring curly maple inlays.
(BladeGallery.com photo)

» JIM POLING:
The san mai bowie struts its nickel silver, stabilized maple, and stainless stuff.
(Mitchell D. Cohen Photography)

» WILL STELTER:
In clad san mai damascus and African blackwood, the cooker is a looker.
(SharpByCoop photo)

FRANCOIS DU TOIT:
Timascus set on titanium liners adds color to the SG2 san mai damascus flipper folder.
(BladeGallery.com photo)

MARK SINCLAIR:
The black and silver san mai blade of the bowie is impressive enough, let alone the stabilized black Mulga wood handle.
(Rod Hoare photo)

JUSTIN CHENAULT:
Such savory san mai damascus steel we have here on a sub-hilt fighter complete with antiqued bronze guard and pommel.
(Mitchell D. Cohen Photography)

SAM REED:
The smokin' hand-forged V-Toku2 san mai blade of the paring knife is counterbalanced by a stabilized wenge wood handle.
(BladeGallery.com photo)

» HERUCUS BLOMERUS:
With a Zircuti handle, clad Takefu SG2 blade and engraving by Gerhard Benade, the flipper folder has class and style to spare.
(SharpByCoop photo)

« JOSHUA FISHER:
The blade of the Kiritsuke chef's knife with mustard Micarta grip is forged from Shiro2 carbon steel between stainless outer layers.
(BladeGallery.com photo)

« BOBBY GARZA:
Equal parts gorgeous are a modified tanto san mai blade and a wooly mammoth ivory handle.
(Caleb Royer photo)

« KURT MERRIKEN:
Clad to the core is a "Mini Ultimatum" folder with a Chad Nichols Boomerang san mai damascus blade, zirconium bolsters, CarboQuartz handle scales, and a copper backspacer and pivot collars.
(Mitchell D. Cohen Photography)

» JULIANO ENDRESS:
The san mai blade of an 8-inch chef's knife combines a 52100 core with stainless sides and is accompanied by an Imbuia burl handle.
(BladeGallery.com photo)

« MARIO GONCALVES:
The san mai blade of the bowie is forged from 5160 carbon steel with 420 stainless sides and given a Jacaranda wood handle.
(BladeGallery.com photo)

« BRIAN BIEGLER:
Rare is the san mai butterfly knife, here in a titanium handle frame with copper carbon-fiber inlays.
(SharpByCoop photo)

Folder Finery

» DELLANA:
Enter the "Sea Dream," a fantasy land of ladder-pattern damascus, 14-karat yellow gold, oxidized and polished sterling silver, rubies, and superb-quality abalone pulled from the maker's pearl hoard. She's been saving it for decades.

(Dellana photo)

» DAVID KULIS:
What a looker—the "Spectre" steps out in a Mike Norris stainless damascus blade, bronze bolsters, curly Koa handle scales, and a Timascus pivot collar and pocket clip.

(Cory Martin photo)

« DAVID LESPECT:
It's not the ironwood handle, the brass bolster, or the wavy temper line of the W1 blade, but the combination of the three that counts.

(SharpByCoop photo)

« A2—ANDRE THORBURN and ANDRE VAN HEERDEN:
The thread running through the front flipper folder is beauty—from its Damasteel blade to the titanium frame with carbon-fiber inlays.

(BladeGallery.com photo)

» STEVE VANDERKOLFF:
I'm not sure what baked musk ox cap handle scales are, but they're the highlight of an otherwise clean CPM 154 slip-joint folder.
(Caleb Royer photo)

» DAVID TABER:
The single-blade CPM 154 tail-lock folder dons its best black and white carbo-quartz attire.
(Cory Martin photo)

« JOHN ARNOLD:
The combination of a stabilized curly Koa handle and a "Copperflake" shred carbon-fiber bolster make the LinerLock folder a nice find.
(BladeGallery.com photo)

⌃ LUKE SWENSON:
Of the split-back seahorse whittler variety, the CPM 154 folder has a gorgeous synthetic shell handle and a gold-inlaid shield.
(Eric Eggly/PointSeven photo)

» ANDERS HEDLUND:
The "Crescent Moon" is a shapely celestial body made up of Damasteel, gold, black-lip pearl, and engraving.
(SharpByCoop photo)

« BRIAN BROWN:
Finery of the "Mini Yeager" frame-lock folder
comes in the form of Mike Norris ladder-
pattern damascus, Blackout Camo
carbon fiber, and a flamed titanium
pocket clip and accents.

(Mitchell D. Cohen Photography)

» CLIFF PARKER:
Fear the Grim Reaper
forged into the mosaic
damascus bolsters of a
mammoth ivory-handle art folder.

(BladeGallery.com photo)

» RICK DUNKERLEY:
A mastodon ivory-handle
damascus folder is scrolled in gold.

(Eric Eggly/PointSeven photo)

» FRANCOIS DU TOIT:
A Damasteel handle frame
with mother-of-pearl inlays gives
a clean and classy look to an RWL-34
flipper folder.

(BladeGallery.com photo)

« KURT MERRIKEN:
The "Mini Karma" locking-liner folder sports a Chad Nichols XHP-core damascus blade, blackened titanium bolsters, and mammoth bark ivory handle scales.

(Mitchell D. Cohen Photography)

» HENNIE DU PLESSIS:
The one-two punch of a locking-liner folder are Damasteel stainless damascus and Gibeon meteorite set on textured and anodized titanium.

(BladeGallery.com photo)

» JAMES INGRAM:
Mammoth ivory and damascus make for a fine locking-liner folder.

(SharpByCoop photo)

« DRAGAN BELJIC:
It's a lock-back folding knife, that of the Damasteel and stabilized spalted beechwood variety.

(Caleb Royer photo)

» BRIAN EFROS:
The "Elder" addresses his tribe in white Timascus handle scales, pocket clip, backspacer and thumb stud, titanium liners, and a CTS XHP blade.

(Mitchell D. Cohen Photography)

« JENSEN BERGMAN:
The chisel-ground brew tool could pop a tab or two, here in a raindrop-damascus recurved tanto blade, and zirconium handle scale with Westinghouse Micarta underlay.

(Mitchell D. Cohen Photography)

« GARETH BULL:
The zirconium handle and Bjorkmans Twist Damasteel blade of the Xyro model equate to subdued elegance.

(SharpByCoop photo)

« RICHARD ROGERS:
A slim utility model is made up of a Damasteel blade, and matrix-pattern zirconium handle inlays.

(Mitchell D. Cohen Photography)

« PRINCETON WONG:
The maker's "Persevere" model is made up of CTS XHP blade steel, titanium, and a sliding scale release mechanism designed by Walt Halucha.

(SharpByCoop photo)

» JERRY MCCLURE:
"Baby Sister" struts around in an EKG damascus blade, textured sterling silver bolsters, and lapis lazuli handle scales.

(Caleb Royer photo)

« PAUL KILBY:
The stunning Alpha folder is dressed in buckeye burl, Damasteel, titanium, zirconium, and copper.

(Mitchell D. Cohen Photography)

« RAFAL BRZESKI:
The full-dress "Shudder" flipper folder steps out in a stainless damascus blade, and a zirconium and titanium handle.

(Eric Eggly/PointSeven photo)

⌃ MARDI MESHEJIAN:
A pair of precision damascus folders, one in a razor-style blade, and the other a Wharncliffe, feature Superconductor and grooved copper bolsters, carbon-fiber handles, titanium liners, and copper back bars.

(SharpByCoop photo)

» DAVID R. (D.R.) DAVIS:
In the locking-liner folder realm is a Mike Norris damascus piece with Robert Eggerling mosaic damascus bolsters, titanium liners, and pearly white handle scales.
(Mitchell D. Cohen Photography)

« TASHI BHARUCHA:
Timascus adds movement to the "Velocity" frame-lock folder.
(Mitchell D. Cohen Photography)

« TOBIN HILL:
There's nothing fancy about the lockback whittler in CPM 154 steel and amber stag handle scales, unless you count fine fit and finish.
(SharpByCoop photo)

» KIRK MAYBERRY:
A slip-lock CPM 154 folder showcases mother-of-pearl handle scales, and Timascus bolsters, backspacer, and clip.
(Mitchell D. Cohen Photography)

« LUCAS BURNLEY:
The frame of the CPM 154 folder is heat colored and milled in a rose motif for a fine effect.
(Mitchell D. Cohen Photography)

» BOB MERZ:
The auto folder is a perfect combination of CPM-154 steel, stainless, and mother-of-pearl.
(SharpByCoop photo)

« PHILIP BOOTH:
The "Bird Break Bomber" auto soars across the horizon in CPM 154 steel, presentation-grade stag, and mosaic damascus.
(Mitchell D. Cohen Photography)

» ANDY ISAACKS:
A gentleman's LinerLock sports a 2.25-inch damascus blade, mammoth ivory handle scales, red spacers, and file-worked and jeweled titanium liners.
(Jocelyn Frasier photo)

« HERUCUS BLOMERUS:
The lines and patterning of the Damasteel and ironwood flipper folder are exquisite.
(SharpByCoop photo)

» MICHAEL WALKER:
Showcasing the maker's BladeLock and multi-alloy Zipper steel, the Crescent model is named for its simplicity in arc and line.

(SharpByCoop photo)

» FRANK EDWARDS:
Extending the feather damascus pattern from the wharncliffe blade onto the bolsters, framing the latter out with gold inlays, and adding mammoth ivory handle scales was all ingenious.

(BladeGallery.com photo)

» IAN TYSON-PICKARSKI:
Four-alloy titanium handle scales further embolden an already stout ORD folder.

(Mitchell D. Cohen Photography)

» PETER MARTIN:
The QSB auto showcases a Lava Lamp damascus blade, black-out superconductor bolsters, and a "Martanium Ti" damascus handle and clip.

(Mitchell D. Cohen Photography)

« TOM KREIN:
Blue mammoth ivory handle scales provide a colorful contrast to the NitroV blade and titanium hardware of an Alpha locking-liner folder.

(Mitchell D. Cohen Photography)

« JOHNNY STOUT:
A color scheme is carried out from the musk ox horn handle to the Dale Bass gold inlay and engraving, and the inlaid thumb stud.

(SharpByCoop photo)

« PETER CAREY:
CarboQuartz handle scales make a statement on the Vertigo model with Mike Norris Hornet's Nest damascus blade.

(Mitchell D. Cohen Photography)

« JAMES BUCKLEY:
The finish of the titanium handle frame "with Vulcan God" elevates the CPM 10V model past standard frame-lock folder fare.

(Mitchell D. Cohen Photography)

» ALEX HOSSOM:
An etched titanium handle takes center stage on a CPM S35VN frame-lock folder.
(Mitchell D. Cohen Photography)

« GUSTAVO CECCHINI:
The brilliant folders sport Balbach Damast and Mike Norris damascus blades, Timascus bolsters and frames, and Timascus, meteorite, and mother-of-pearl handles.
(SharpByCoop photo)

» RON BEST:
Why stop at one version of a Damasteel, pearl, and titanium folding tanto when you can build two?
(SharpByCoop photo)

» CHARLES GEDRAITIS:
The R2-D2-themed Swiss Army Knife-style switchblade is done up in a Damasteel blade, a G-10 frame and handle scales, and a black pearl "eye."
(SharpByCoop photo)

» JOEY KIDO:
The Cadence LinerLock creates harmony via a Magnacut blade, and milled and anodized titanium frame, hardware and overlays.
(Mitchell D. Cohen Photography)

» JEREMY MARSH:
In case there was any confusion about who built the CPM 154 frame-lock folder, Steel Flame etched Marsh's "M" logo across the titanium handle.
(Mitchell D. Cohen Photography)

« CHUCK COOK:
Dyed camel bone is the copacetic handle material of choice for the 208-layer damascus folder with a nickel-silver bolster.
(SharpByCoop photo)

» JONAS IGLESIAS:
The Mike Norris "Hornet's Nest" damascus blade and red/black CarboQuartz handle scales work perfectly together.
(Mitchell D. Cohen Photography)

« STANLEY BUZEK:
The two-blade damascus and mammoth ivory folder features an acorn shield and engraved and gold-inlaid bolsters by Alice Carter.
(SharpByCoop photo)

Deep-Cut Damascus

Taking a deep dive into damascus is a commitment to spending hours at the forge, hammering steel, folding, beating, heating, and repeating. The patterns don't even emerge until hours and even days later when the steel is finally finished, etched, and polished.

So, is the reward worth the risk? Readers of the KNIVES 2024 book can be the judge of that, but in the author's opinion, the skill of the bladesmiths is evident in every inch of pattern-welded steel displayed on this and the following pages. Not only are no two patterns alike, but most are tightly controlled, well-thought-out and planned, and perfectly executed examples of their genre.

It takes an initial deep dive to eventually emerge with these deep-cut damascus beauties, and such efforts rarely go unnoticed by buyers, users, and casual observers who can't help but admire the intricacies of the bladesmiths' work.

» LEE LERMAN:
The blade shape of the bolster-lock flipper folder and the finished flats highlight the Chad Nichols Intrepid stainless damascus.
(Mitchell D. Cohen Photography)

« MACE VITALE:
It might be a no-frills fixed blade, but the wrought iron and damascus blade, and maple and silver handle are equally impressive.
(SharpByCoop photo)

« ANTON VAN DER WESTHUIZEN:
There's no mistaking Bertie Rietveld heat-colored "Dragonskin" damascus, here on a front flipper with a Timascus frame and meteorite inlays.
(BladeGallery.com photo)

《 BRUCE BARNETT:
"Smiling Sharkstooth" damascus does triple duty on a lock-back whittler with mother-of-pearl handle scales.
(SharpByCoop photo)

《 KELLY VERMEER-VELLA:
A "Riptide" damascus blade pulls you in, and then pushes you out to sea clinging to that mammoth ivory handle.
(Eric Eggly/PointSeven photo)

《 CHARLES CARPENTER:
A "Texas Wind W's" damascus blade adds some freshness to a bowie with a hammered steel spacer and blackwood handle.
(Caleb Royer photo)

《 CLAUDIO and ARIEL SOBRAL/CAS KNIVES:
The multi-ground, sculpted damascus blade with integral guard and arching fuller is perfectly paired with wood handle scales.
(SharpByCoop photo)

《 CHRIS GISH:
"Wave Pool" damascus is a perfectly appropriate name for the patterning, forged by Chad Nichols, of a chisel-ground integral fixed blade with a cord-wrapped grip.
(Mitchell D. Cohen Photography)

《 STEVE DUNN:
The aptly named "waterfall" damascus blade spills out from an engraved guard and sambar stag handle.
(BladeGallery.com photo)

« JERRY FISK:
As if the stunning multi-pattern damascus blade weren't enough, the handle of the prizefighter is made up of two woods—one from a tree planted by George Washington, and the second from the original post that held the Liberty Bell.
(SharpByCoop photo)

« MIKE QUESENBERRY
The incredible pattern of the Turkish twist damascus blade can be approached only by the exhibition-grade stag handle.
(Eric Eggly/PointSeven photo)

« JOSE SANTIAGO-CUMMINGS:
With an Alabama Damascus blade that reminds one of a topographical map, the cook's knife also incorporates mokume-gane, buffalo horn, abalone, composite lapis lazuli, mahogany, and mastodon ivory.
(Caleb Royer photo)

« BERTIE RIETVELD:
Dragonskin damascus dares the observer to look past it towards the charcoal jade handle and Jonathan Knoesen gold inlay.
(SharpByCoop photo)

» JERRY MCCLURE:
Impressive features of "Baby Sister" include a 1095-and-15N20-damascus blade forged by the maker, a sterling silver handle fused with 22-karat gold, and gold Dellana dots. It's built with the maker's jeweled pivot of eight rubies.
(SharpByCoop photo)

« NEELS VAN DEN BERG:
The dynamite ring dagger exhibits a "Twist Explosion" damascus blade, fluted red bush willow burl handle with twisted silver wire wrap, and aged bronze hardware.
(Eric Eggly/PointSeven photo)

« DAVID TUTHILL:
The "Mountain Sky"-pattern damascus blade of the Gyuto chef's knife is as impressive as its name, and accompanied by a Macassar ebony handle and buffalo horn bolster.
(BladeGallery.com photo)

« STEPHAN FOWLER:
The zebra damascus blade looks like it can chomp through some tall grasses, doesn't it? The mammoth ivory handle makes its presence known.
(SharpByCoop photo)

« SHAYNE CARTER:
The mammoth ivory-handle hunter features a dynamite damascus blade.
(SharpByCoop photo)

» IAN TYSON-PICKARSKI:
The Chad Nichols "Intrepid" damascus blade and micro carbon-fiber handle scales nearly match on the Mini Icarus V2 LinerLock.
(Mitchell D. Cohen Photography)

« TODD REXFORD:
In addition to the ebbing and flowing damascus blade, the NM1B model showcases a hardened stainless frame with hot-hammered zirconium inlays throughout, as well as a V2 RDLM locking module system made from stainless damascus.
(Mitchell D. Cohen Photography)

« DAN TOMPKINS:
Wearing its damascus blade like a tattoo, the chef's knife also exhibits an aluminum bronze bolster and ancient bog oak handle.
(SharpByCoop photo)

⌃ ADAM MILLE:
The recurved blade of a quilted maple-handle hunter is 1084 and 15N20 damascus.
(SharpByCoop photo)

⌃ ANDREW MEERS:
Follow the light squiggly line along the damascus blade of the fighter, straight to the African blackwood handle and back again.
(SharpByCoop photo)

» HENNING WILKINSON:
Highly figured wood combined with intricate damascus patterning brings an integral keyhole hunter to life.
(SharpByCoop photo)

« CODY ADOLPHSON:
The Firestorm damascus blade of the chef's knife should heat up things in the kitchen, and equally hot is the spalted maple handle with meteorite spacer.
(Jocelyn Frasier image)

« MARK BARRETT:
The Turkish twist damascus blade of the bread knife is attached to a York gum burl handle with a stippled resin-based Juma spacer.
(Rod Hoare photo)

« SETH LOPEZ:
Designed by Steve Schwarzer, the Royal Chopper is orchestrated in 1084-and-15N20 damascus, African blackwood, and copper.
(SharpByCoop photo)

« PETER MARTIN:
Bubble damascus makes a statement on the QSB flipper folder in a gold-lip mother-of-pearl handle.
(Cory Martin photo)

« SAM LURQUIN:
Featuring a "twist explosion" damascus blade forged by the maker and Sylvain Dix-Neuf, the sub-hilt fighter also showcases a presentation ironwood handle and engraving by Elizabeth Da Justa. It comes with a Jeremy Guillaume leather sheath.

(SharpByCoop photo)

» HENNING WILKINSON:
The HHH lightning damascus blade of the "Revenge" contrasts beautifully with the Koa handle and mosaic pins.

(Mitchell D. Cohen Photography)

« JEREMY BARTLETT:
That damascus blade is the star of a stag-handle hunter.

(Mitchell D. Cohen Photography)

« CHRIS SHARP:
Aside from a deep-cut 1080-and-15N20 damascus blade, the slip-joint folder features an amber stag handle and the maker's patented pierced and inlaid shield.

(SharpByCoop photo)

» CHRIS DREW:
The combination of Salem Straub damascus and shredded carbon fiber shreds it.

(Caleb Royer photo)

« MICHAEL VAGNINO:
Situational cutting need is everything when it comes to the dynamic damascus blade that locks open in the traditional folder or push dagger positions. Mild steel bolsters and mammoth ivory handle scales complete the piece.

(SharpByCoop photo)

» ENRIQUE PINA:
The lines are drawn on an integral damascus bird's-beak garnish/paring knife with stabilized curly mango wood handle.

(BladeGallery.com photo)

« JOEL WORLEY:
It's hard to imagine a more beautiful knife than the keyhole dirk in Turkish Twist W's-pattern damascus, integral bolsters, and a sculpted cocobolo handle.

(Mitchell D. Cohen Photography)

« BRIAN NAWROCKI:
A spear-point fighter endears itself via a Bob Rankin damascus blade, nickel silver guard, and fossil walrus ivory handle.

(SharpByCoop photo)

« JAYDEN SIMISKY:
A take-down piece and collaboration with Ryan Searls and Lewis Evans, the GoMai blade is forged from wrought iron, pure nickel and 1095, and held to the 6AL4V titanium handle by a series of copper pins and washers, and a single damascus pin.

(SharpByCoop photo)

« RUSSELL ROOSEVELT:
Take a deep dive into the damascus and spalted maple burl bowie, that with coined stainless spacers.

(SharpByCoop photo)

» TYLER TURNER:
The everyday carry prototype is defined by a full-tang Damasteel blade with matching shield, red liners, Norplex ivory G-10 handle scales, and domed Argentium silver pins with diamond insets.

(Mitchell D. Cohen Photography)

» BRENT STUBBLEFIELD:
The nine-inch multi-bar damascus blade is etched and finished perfectly, accented by an explosion damascus bolster and redwood burl handle.

(Caleb Royer photo)

« AARON WILBURN:
Like barbed wire against animal fur, the deep-cut damascus patterning commands attention on an ivory-handle hunter.

(SharpByCoop photo)

« RYAN SCHWARTZ:
Ocean-blue hues of Fat Carbon complement the pooling Chad Nichols "Black Hole" damascus blade.

(Mitchell D. Cohen Photography)

« LUCAS BURNLEY:
Amenities of the frame-lock folder include a Thor-pattern Damasteel blade, titanium frame, and Fat Carbon inlays.

(Mitchell D. Cohen Photography)

» JON MOORE:
This bust-out bowie blends a "Mechanical" damascus blade with a fire-red honeycomb handle, stainless fittings, and a crocodile skin sheath.

« LUKE SWENSON:
The way the maker matched the damascus shield to the blades is a stroke of genius in a three-blade, stag-handle pocketknife embodying good ideas.
(Mitchell D. Cohen Photography)

« ANDREW GEASLIN:
The seax knife integrates an Emiliano Carrillo multi-bar damascus blade, a bone and bronze guard, and a snakewood handle.
(SharpByCoop photo)

« JIM POOR:
The devil's in the details of a "Voodoo" damascus blade on an oosic-handle fighter.
(BladeGallery.com photo)

« TASHI BHARUCHA:
The flipper folder is nearly entirely fashioned from Sam Lurquin damascus, but for the titanium liners, and zirconium backspacer.
(SharpByCoop photo)

⌃ TOM MAYO:
The "Doctor Death" fixed blade and "TNT" folder set makes ample use of Rob Thomas Spirograph damascus.
(Mitchell D. Cohen Photography)

» LUIZ GUSTAVO GONCALVES:
The integral damascus chef's knife parades a hand-forged 15N20-and-1095 damascus blade and a hand-sculpted stabilized maple burl grip.
(BladeGallery.com photo)

» JASON FRY:
This one's literally been through battle—the 324-layer damascus blade forged from Battleship Texas gun turret bearings as well as Okinawa shrapnel, the guard and frame from a Battleship Texas plate, and the handle fashioned from a Battleship Texas longleaf pine deck board.
(SharpByCoop photo)

« MAURICIO DALETZKY:
A River of Fire damascus blade helps define the presentation criollo knife, along with gold inlays, engraving, a blued steel pommel, and a carbon-fiber handle.
(SharpByCoop photo)

Golden Touches

« BILL TUCH:
It doesn't get much more golden than knife handle engraving by Rick Simmons of the Beatles walking across Abbey Road.
(Mitchell D. Cohen Photography)

« LUIZ GUSTAVO GONCALVES:
Golden touches on an integral hunter include a Turkish twist-pattern damascus blade and guard, mammoth ivory handle scales, and gold inlays.
(BladeGallery.com photo)

« RICK DUNKERLEY:
He took gold leaf to a whole new level on the blued-damascus art folder with carved mother-of-pearl handle.
(Eric Eggly/PointSeven photo)

» ANDREW BLOMFIELD:
A Turkish twist damascus Indo-Persian-style pesh-kabz model sports a mammoth ivory handle and gold engraving and inlay work by the maker. Cue the mic drop already.
(SharpByCoop photo)

« JERRY MCCLURE:
"Little Mama" sashays her damascus blade, 24k-gold-infused sterling silver handle, and 3-millimeter black cherry diamond thumb stud.
(SharpByCoop photo)

« BUSTER WARENSKI:
The frame of the late, great Buster Warenski's dress locking folder is engraved with gold inlays, framing black-lip mother-of-pearl inlays and engraved bolsters.
(SharpByCoop photo)

« JOHNNY STOUT:
Golden flowers dot the stainless frame of an Alice Carter-engraved "Baron" art folder with cracked mammoth ivory handle inlays and an Owen Wood damascus blade.
(SharpByCoop photo)

« STANLEY BUZEK:
The two-blade Texas trapper exhibits Mike Tyre damascus, blue mammoth ivory, and Alice Carter gold inlay and engraving.
(SharpByCoop photo)

» ANDERS HEDLUND:
The aptly named "Fortune Fighter" features gold inlay and engraving across the RWL-34 steel blade and handle frame, interrupted only by a checkered black lip mother-of-pearl inlay.
(SharpByCoop photo)

» JIM SORNBERGER:
Kicking off the ATS-34 San Francisco dagger are gold quartz handle inlays, and a gold handle frame engraved by the maker. The fine art knife comes with an engraved silver sheath.
(Mitchell D. Cohen Photography)

≽ HARVEY DEAN:
There's gold and engraving in that Coke bottle dagger, along with "Texas Tornado" damascus and antique tortoise shell.
(SharpByCoop photo)

« DENNIS FRIEDLY:
In celebration of his 50th year of knifemaking, the maker had Ray Cover Jr. add a little gold inlay and engraving onto a mammoth ivory-handle fighter.
(SharpByCoop photo)

≪ DELLANA:
The master of oozing, dripping, cracked gold bolsters builds such a folder in a pearl handle and ladder-pattern damascus blade.
(Dellana photo)

« DWAYNE DUSHANE:
It never ceases to amaze when the makers forge the blades, engrave the knives, and inlay them with gold and mastodon ivory, all being of sole authorship.
(SharpByCoop photo)

» JERRY FISK:
The small bowie packs a big punch in the form of a multi-bar damascus blade with 24k-gold flame overlays, a mammoth ivory handle, and deep relief gold inlay and engraving. (SharpByCoop photo)

« FRANK EDWARDS:
Gold wire inlays follow the spiraling scroll pattern of the engraved nitro-colored steel handle scales on a damascus folding dagger. (Jocelyn Frasier photo)

« TYLER TURNER:
Twenty-four-karat gold inlays by Jody Muller beautify the black G-10-handle CTS-XHP fixed blade. (SharpByCoop photo)

» TOM OVEREYNDER:
An Amayak Stepanyan design, the golden goodness includes Joe Mason engraving enveloping a Deschutes jasper handle inlay, and a long fuller groove in the PSF-27 blade. SharpByCoop photo)

« DANIELE IBBA:
It's a "Triumph" alright, in Dario Quartini mosaic damascus, lapis lazuli, and Fabio Bregoli gold inlay and engraving. (SharpByCoop photo)

Edgy Ladder Patterns

» MATTHEW PARKINSON:
Winner of the 2022 American Bladesmith Society Moran Award, the bowie boasts a 400-layer ladder-pattern damascus blade, nickel silver guard, and a silver wire-inlaid maple handle.
(SharpByCoop photo)

« CODY HOFSOMMER:
The maker needed a long, recurved laddered W-pattern blade, guard, and sub-hilt to compete with the ringed Gidgee grip.
(Cory Martin photo)

« BEN AKIN:
Rungs of the ladder-W's pattern climb the entire length of the damascus blade, from the curly maple handle with mammoth molar spacer to the very tip.
(Jocelyn Frasier photo)

« BRUCE BARNETT:
Forged from 1084 and 15N20 carbon steels, the ladder-pattern damascus blade of the saddle-horn lock-back folder cuts the mustard, as does the black Mulga wood handle.
(BladeGallery.com photo)

« ZANE DVORAK:
Everything about the hunter is edgy, from the high-contrast ladder-pattern damascus blade to the integral bolster and maple burl handle.
(Mitchell D. Cohen Photography)

« PHILIP YLITALO:
Anchored by a dyed and stabilized cottonwood grip, the kitchen knife sports a nickel silver and bronze bolster, and long ladder-pattern damascus blade.
(Cory Martin photo)

» BRUCE SCHUBERT:
A 100-layer ladder-pattern damascus blade pulls duty on a bird-and-trout knife with nickel silver duckbill guard and stabilized Jarrah burl handle.
(Rod Hoare photo)

⌃ JASON KRAUS:
Between the ladder-pattern damascus blade, wrought iron guard, and curly redwood handle, the Jouet Cher bowie is a high-end toy.
(SharpByCoop photo)

» LIN RHEA:
Ladder-pattern damascus contrasts nicely with the fossil walrus ivory grip of the 15.25-inch bowie.
(Jocelyn Frasier photo)

Classic Carving

» ANDREW BLOMFIELD:
A carved ringed Gidgee handle invites onlookers to pick up the sub-hilt bowie and flash the 1095 blade a time or two. (BladeGallery.com photo)

« FRANCK SOUVILLE:
Equally at home in the tiki hut or church picnic, the damascus folder features a mammoth ivory handle colossally carved by Alex Dubois. (SharpByCoop photo)

» SCOTT SWEDER:
Carved in buffalo horn and antler, the raven that makes up the handle of the feather damascus fixed blade has lapis lazuli eyes. (Eric Eggly/PointSeven photo)

« PAUL DISTEFANO:
Not your ordinary hunter/utility knife, the mosaic damascus model parades its carved box elder burl handle for all to admire. (SharpByCoop photo)

» JEAN-PIERRE POTVIM:
The ash wood grip of
the "Spear of Warrior"
is tastefully carved to
accompany a brass-copper
mokume-gane bolster, and
damascus point.

« RICK DUNKERLEY:
Carved tortoise shell handle scales,
engraved bolsters and gold inlays
embellish a six-blade damascus folder.
(Eric Eggly/PointSeven photo)

« TOMMY CARROLL:
The 5160 "Engagement Sword"
showcases a betrothed couple carved
into the elk bone handle and has a silver
ring set into the pommel.
(Eric Eggly/PointSeven photo)

FACTORY TRENDS

N ot only are the blade steels, handle materials, and in the case of folders, mechanisms, pivots, and locks high tech, but modern factory knives are also representing the newest and hottest patterns of knives, those popular with youth and seasoned knife enthusiasts.

Those who've spent more than a few decades on this planet can remember when production knives had simple high-carbon or stainless blades, all in a handful of alloys available in bulk to knife companies, and handle materials consisted of whatever wood, pearl, or synthetic material was inexpensive and would last.

Times changed quickly, and to keep pace, manufacturers hired in-house metallurgists to study the newest performance steels, machinists to figure out ways to cut, hone and finish the alloys, and designers to come up with new patterns, mechanisms, pivots, features, sheaths, springs, gadgets, locks, clips, notches, openers, and carry methods.

It took years for factories to catch up with custom knifemakers in the technology sector, and many manufacturers collaborated with and even hired makers of handmade knives. Eventually factories began offering knives in every price category for users of every skill and knowledge level. Some of the most amazing production knives have come out of manufacturing lines over the past two decades.

So, what was next on the horizon? Thinking outside the box. Today knife factories offer many of the same styles of knives that have become popular on the internet and with bloggers, influencers, and on YouTube, Snapchat, Instagram, and Facebook.

Once-traditional knife companies are offering butterfly knives, bushcraft blades, flipper folders, refined gent's knives, and crossover kitchen/field knives, or those with carabiners for clipping to any part of your clothing or outdoor gear. It's an exciting time to be a knife enthusiast, and technology is speeding up, not slowing down.

WHERE TACTICALS GOT THEIR EDGES

The author traces the origins of today's varied, unusual, and exotic blade shapes.

By Pat Covert

The knife industry has experienced some incredible innovations over the last quarter century, among them advanced locking mechanisms, new blade opening systems, and super steels. Nothing, however, defines a knife like its blade, and the modern tactical era has turned the cutlery world on edge, so to speak.

The type of knife, whether fixed blade or folder, is typically the first purchasing decision a buyer or end user considers, but once the format has been determined, it's the style of blade that hooks an enthusiast.

Most of us have blade styles we find ultimately appealing, and our choice is often determined by the knife's intended use. The modern tactical era spurred custom knifemakers and manufacturers to rethink blade styles for a couple of reasons. Because designers are curious by nature, they wanted to try new things, be more effective, and push the envelope. Secondly, a

revival in tactical knives quickly became competitive, so standing out in the crowd was the challenge.

Typically, custom knifemakers have driven innovation, while the role of manufacturers has largely been to adopt trends and technologies, adapt them into a production setting, and offer customers more affordable versions of handmade blades. In recent years, manufacturers have increasingly collaborated with custom knifemakers on production designs. These collaborations between the custom makers and factories became quite common and are a mainstay today.

The evolution of the edge has brought about many interesting changes to the knife world and spurred sub-genres of blade styles. For instance, EDC (everyday carry) knives have made huge inroads within the folding knife market to the point of becoming their own category separate from tactical pieces. Some EDC knives are considered ideal for self-defense and protec-

Released over 25 years ago, CRKT's Kit Carson-designed M16 and its many spinoffs exemplify the modern folding knife. At top is an M16 with tanto blade and below it is an M14 spear point.

CRKT teamed with famed retailer A.G. Russell Knives to produce the Sting III Boot Dagger shown here. The dagger is one of the oldest blade styles, dating back to prehistoric times.

tion, others remain more utilitarian, and crossover pieces borrow design elements from each.

Just about all blade styles have benefitted from a boom in design and technology. Let's look at some of these innovative designs.

Dagger and spear-point patterns date back to the Stone Age when the practice of knapping flint eventually produced handheld, hafted blades. Through the sands of time, early knapped blades became our modern daggers and spear points, with daggers typically being double-edged, and spear points having a similar symmetrical profile with a couple of key differences. Daggers tend to be slimmer and relegated to combat while spear points are generally wider, therefore offering more utility. Yet, there is some overlap between the two.

With narrow profiles and set symmetrical designs, innovation in modern daggers and spear points comes in the form of assisted-opening or automatic/switchblade mechanisms, and progressive design elements that have generally evolved for all fixed blades and folders.

Drop-Point Blade

The drop-point blade style, on the other hand, is asymmetrical, with a deeper curve on the cutting edge and a gently sloping spine. Drop-point blades are extremely popular today, and although their design, too, likely dates to prehistoric times, the style got a huge boost in popularity from hunting knives of the late, great Bob Loveless. An effective design for field dressing and processing game, the drop-point blade remains a favorite of hunters while also being adopted by tactical users for its versatility in the field.

Most recently, drop points have been modified in various ways, mainly to improve hand purchase with design touches like finger choils, ramped thumb rests, grooved jimping on the spines, and in some instances,

The Kershaw Deschutes Skinner is a thoroughly modern drop point, replete with a deep finger choil, jimping on the blade spine, and a modern, green, molded polypropylene handle. At bottom is a replica of a Texas corner tang flint-knapped blade.

Benchmade's Crooked River model (top) is a state-of-the-art clip-point folding hunter with thumb stud openers and a modern Axis Lock. Even the most famous folding hunter of all time, the Buck 110 first produced in the 1960s, got converted to an automatic (bottom).

Two modern trailing points are shown here. At top is the Doublestar Chico Diablo tactical with a harpoon-style thumb rest, and below it is a Spyderco streamlined Bow River hunter.

a combination of such elements. The blade design has also been adapted to a variety of handles from simple stick or slab styles to those with finger grooves for improved grip. The drop point has turned into one of the most versatile and popular blades today.

Clip points are highly popular, and trailing points not as much, but there's a connection between the two. The clip-point blade design has a downward break at its spine that slopes to the point, making it ideal for penetration. Many bowies sport clip-point blades for their ability to stab and penetrate without sacrificing slicing effectiveness. Eventually, this blade style made it onto folding knives and was found to be effective for skinning game.

The Buck 110 folding hunter is a perfect example of the clip point's usefulness and was the first folder of its kind to be widely embraced by hunters. Modern tactical knife users have employed the clip point on fixed blades and folders for the same reasons the design became a staple of the bowie—it can penetrate and slice. Some bowies sport curved clips like mini-trailing points, a style that has also found a place on folders.

Also referred to as a Persian blade, the trailing point curves continuously upward from handle to tip, conjuring up images of swashbuckling swords like scimitars and cutlasses. In fact, as sword fighting became mostly obsolete with the introduction of firearms, there was still a need for a large blade. The bowie, a knife that could equally pull camp and combat duty, became common thanks in large part to its legendary namesake, Col. James Bowie. Although the frontiersman's original bowie used in the Sandbar Fight is reputed to have been a modified

The RMJ Tactical Korbin Karambit is a version of the Indonesian fighting knife boiled down to its simplest wicked form. Modern karambits vary widely, with folding versions becoming all the rage lately.

butcher knife, the pattern began to be offered in a wide variety of blade styles, with the clip point being the most popular. Standing the test of time, clip points and trailing points have been modified for modern tactical and EDC knives.

Straight-edged blades such as sheepsfoot and wharncliffe folding-knife patterns have experienced a modern revival. The sheepsfoot style is the older of the two and was commonly employed as a utility blade on folding knives for chores like cutting rope and stripping electrical wire. The wharncliffe would come later as an alternative to the sheepsfoot. Not as common in the straight-edge blade genre are lamb's-foot and coping patterns.

The wharncliffe got a huge boost in the tactical arena when martial artist and combat knife instructor Michael Janich experimented with the pattern and determined it ideal for self-defense applications. Janich collaborated with Spyderco Knife Company to produce the wharncliffe Ronin and Yojimbo models. In my opinion, Janich single-handedly created the wharncliffe niche of the tactical knife market, spurring Spyderco to produce more versions of the knives such as folding Yojimbo models. Custom knifemakers and other manufacturers followed suit, and the wharncliffe is now common fare.

The Viking seax is a short sword design that has been resurrected for tactical use. Historically, there have been different versions of the blade, some completely flat along the edges, and others with a slight curve. All had spines that jutted down abruptly toward the tip. Most notably, Emerson Knives has produced fixed-blade and folding versions of the seax, each with a slight, almost imperceptible curve along the edge.

Hawkbill Karambits

While the hawkbill blade has been a part of many cultures, including our own here in the United States, nowhere have we seen such an explosion of the pattern as on Indonesian-style karambit fighting knives. Like many blade styles, the Indonesian karambit had humble beginnings. Used primarily as a farm tool in the 1100s, the ring-handled, hooked blade spread

Here we have two combat folders designed by a pair of accomplished martial artists. The Emerson Seax is a modern take on its namesake Viking fixed blade, and at bottom sits a Michael Janich-designed Spyderco Yojimbo 2 with a highly stylized wharncliffe blade.

The modern bushcraft movement embraced the Scandinavian puukko due to its woodworking prowess. The Kellam Jouni 70 at top is a traditionally styled puukko. Knifemaker Bob Dozier modified his Bushcrafter with a drop-point blade and a simpler, bolster-less handle (bottom).

to other countries in Southeast Asia and eventually worked its way into the broader martial arts arena for which the area has become legendary.

Karambits were rediscovered in the modern tactical era as another style of fighting knives, and rightfully so. The vicious beak-like blades are ripping and tearing machines. Manufacturers have climbed on board with fixed-blade and folding karambits. The hawkbill blade style has been employed to tackle many chores in the knife world, from pruning trees and bushes to cutting linoleum. Though never achieving the sheer popularity of the karambit, custom knifemakers and manufacturers alike have adopted the hawkbill design for use on tactical knives, and utility versions of the blade can still be found.

The Japanese tanto has also made its presence known in the modern tactical arena, not surprisingly for its strong, chisel-ground, penetrating tip. Japanese tantos from warring times of the 12th century differed from the fare we see today in that they typically had short upward-curving tips as opposed to the abrupt angles popular today. This has prompted some to call the current blade style a Western tanto. The chisel grind with one-sided bevel on some modern tantos is not original to the knife, but rather lifted from a style used on Japanese culinary knives.

The stout tanto excels at puncturing, penetrating, and slicing, so it was only natural that it should emerge at the forefront of modern tactical knives. Though not an ideal utility blade, the tanto more than suffices as an EDC for self-defense. The big change in

tantos has been in folding knives by custom knifemakers and manufacturers alike who, to this day, include them in their offerings.

The puukko, originally attributed to Finnish knifemakers, is considered a Scandinavian knife purpose-built for everyday hunting and fishing chores. This knife, known for its simple barrel-shaped handle, straight blade spine, and shallow V-ground Scandi edge, was borne not out of the modern tactical era. Rather, it emerged from the increasingly popular, contemporary bushcraft movement that started in England and came to our shores approximately 15 years ago. Known for its apt woodworking abilities, the puukko sparked a revival in current factory fare

Hawkbills like the Rite Edge throwback at top were mainly pruning knives until the modern tactical era. The Spyderco Tasmin Salt, shown at bottom, has a wicked serrated blade that could serve for both self-protection and emergency rescue.

The Spyderco Caribbean Salt (top) has a modern sheepsfoot blade, albeit modified with a slightly curved edge. Contrast it with an old-style Schrade Rope knife (bottom). I have heard the latter referred to as a "coping sheepsfoot."

and soon knifemakers and manufacturers took to it. Today, modernized bushcraft knives have definite puukko design influences but with different blade grinds, more ergonomic handles, and a wide variety of high-carbon and stainless steels.

Other blade styles that have become fashionable but not prominent enough to command a huge market share still deserve mention. Take, for instance, the cleaver and straight razor-style blades popular today and that have found a place in the

tactical knife market. Manufacturers are all over the board when they define these knives. Cleavers are often referred to as straight razors, but the easiest way to tell the difference is by the height or depth of the blade from spine to edge. If deep, it's more like a cleaver. If shallow, the style is closer to that of a straight razor. To confuse the issue, old-time cleavers had small holes in the blades so they could be hung from hooks, but in some cases today this addition has found its way onto straight razors. And, yes, some modern practitioners shave with the razors!

The harpoon-style blade is another trend in modern knifemaking. The prominent raised-clip style of blade swoops up from the thumb rest to meet a raised main spine. The harpoon style works well with a drop- or trailing-point tip, making for one wicked-looking blade. Unlike a typical barbed harpoon, the blade spine serves better as a thumb ramp than something you'd expect to snag a speared fish. Nevertheless, it does make for an impressive pattern that some simply refer to as a harpoon blade.

Still other blade twists include the reverse tanto with an upside-down chisel tip, and modified wharncliffe that has a slight belly to the blade. Re-curved blade edges have been offered up enough to become trendy as well, and serrations have been around enough to become nearly passé or old hat.

Are we in the heyday of blade design, or has the trend toward multitudes of interesting patterns peaked? Don't count out blade innovation in the future. Knifemakers and manufacturers have never been ones to stop advancing, adopting what has worked in the past and adapting it to modern times. □

These two swayback jacks with wharncliffe blades are both new, but very different. At top is Spyderco's send up in a titanium handle with a frame-lock mechanism, and at bottom is A.G. Russell's traditional slip joint featuring stainless steel bolsters and smooth white bone scales.

Straight razors and cleaver blades have gone from shaving and meal prep to full-tilt tactical in recent years. At top is the Gerber Flatiron razor, and below are Buckshot and Spyderco cleavers.

BARE ESSENTIAL BUSHCRAFT BLADES

The solid bushcraft knives on this page include, from top to bottom, the Casstrom No. 10 Swedish Forest Knife, TOPS Knives Fieldcraft by Brothers of Bushcraft, and White River Knife & Tool FC-PKO. All have high-tech stainless blades and Micarta handles.

(Josh Wayner image)

From left to right, the Flexcut Explorer, Condor Darklore, Benchmade Anonimus, and ESEE 3 S35VN fixed blades exude modern bushcraft makeup and design. While the Darklore's country of origin is El Salvador, it exhibits a 1095 high-carbon steel blade and black paper Micarta handle. The other three are made in the USA, and feature zebrawood (Explorer), and G-10 (Anonimus and ESEE 3) handles. Like Darklore, the Explorer sports a 1095 blade, and the Anonimus and ESEE 3 employ CPM CruWear tool steel and CPM S35VN stainless blades, respectively. *(Pat Covert image)*

HOT AND FRESH FLIPPER FOLDERS

⌃ The stonewashed blade of the Kershaw Inception pivots on KVT ball bearings. The custom pivot collar adds a touch of class.

» The Full Track Spearpoint "Nuked" has a removable tool seated in the spine for disassembly/assembly of the knife. The scale on the show side is removable to store spare washers and spacers.

« The CPM S35VN stainless blade of the Medford Fighter Flipper is 3/16-inch thick at the thickest and has a Rockwell hardness of 58 HRC.

» The Sliverax is the first factory folder to combine Spyderco's Compression Lock® with a flipper-style opener. Blade thickness and grind: .138 inch at the thickest and full flat.

BALISONGS FLY LIKE BUTTERFLIES

« Being an accomplished Balisong flipper seems to come with the territory at Squid Industries, as Andre Mayo, the company's assembly manager, likes to demonstrate the Squid Teal Krake Raken Bowie V2.5 for customers.

« According to Vance Collver, Benchmade director of product line management, the Benchmade 85 Billet Ti Bali-Song is not available in a trainer version and is for experienced flippers only. It includes a convenient carry pouch.

« "Having the critical dimensions of a balisong in place combined with a well-tuned bushing system makes for the best flipping experience," stated Edward Anthonis of Bladerunner Systems. The Premium Alpha Beast Kukri from Bladerunner features such a bushing system.

⌃ The Kershaw Moonsault 5050 is copiously skeletonized to help reduce the weight of the stainless steel handles. Weight: 6.1 ounces

REFINED GENT'S KNIVES

⌄ The Case Tear Drop Black Sea Dichrolam spear-point blade is designed with a strong tip for piercing, which comes in handy for such gent's knife jobs as opening mail, packages, and the like.

⌃ The polyhedral tungsten carbide blade of the Sandrin Torino is designed to retain its razor-sharp edge far beyond that of steel blades in Sandrin's "StaySharp Technology."

⌃ Designed by custom knifemakers Jesper Vox and Jens Anso, the GiantMouse ACE Nibbler holds fast via a reversible wire clip.

⌃ The thoughtfully designed deep carry clip and the thin, lightweight nature of the Pro-Tech Newport 3405 make it a good choice for wearing dress slacks, as it won't tear up the pocket or be heavy enough to make it sag.

KNIVES WITH CARABINERS HANG TOUGH

Carabiners are handy built-in accessories that offer clip-on ways to carry knives such as, from left to right, the DPX Heat Hiker, Fox Knives Ferox, Kershaw Reverb XL, and CRKT Compano Sheepsfoot. *(Pat Covert image)*

FOOD AND FIELD KNIVES

Knives that cross over from field to kitchen and back include, from left to right, two sizes of the Spyderco Utility Knife with different edge configurations, the White River Knife & Tool Exodus 4, and two sizes of TOPS Knives Frog Market Specials. *(Josh Wayner image)*

KNIFEMAKERS INDEX

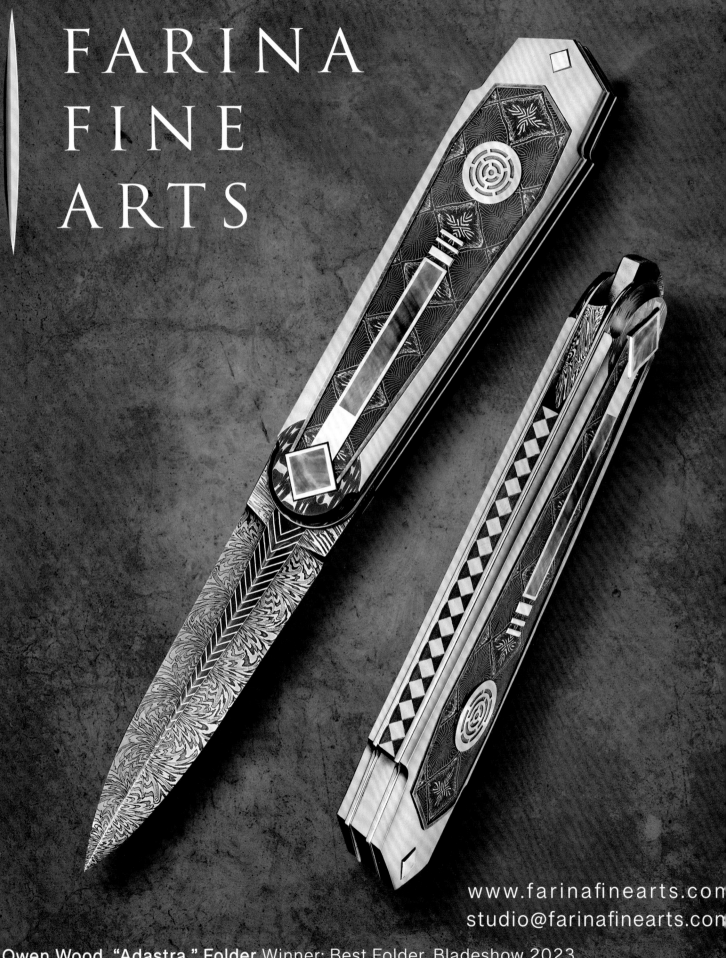

FARINA FINE ARTS

Owen Wood, "Adastra," Folder Winner: Best Folder, Bladeshow 2023

Sole Authorship, Blade: 3 piece composite herringbone & explosion pattern damascus; Scales: 416 stainless; Mosaic damascu
Liners: 6Al4V Titanium; Primary inlay frame: Copper; Secondary Inlays: Mosaic damascus; Tertiary inlays: Gold; Quaternary
inlays; Blacklip pearl; Spacer: 416 stainless; Additional edm decoration
Photography by Ricardo Velarde

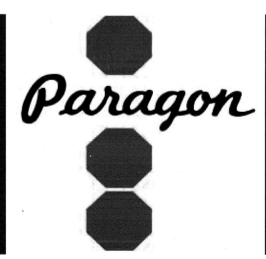

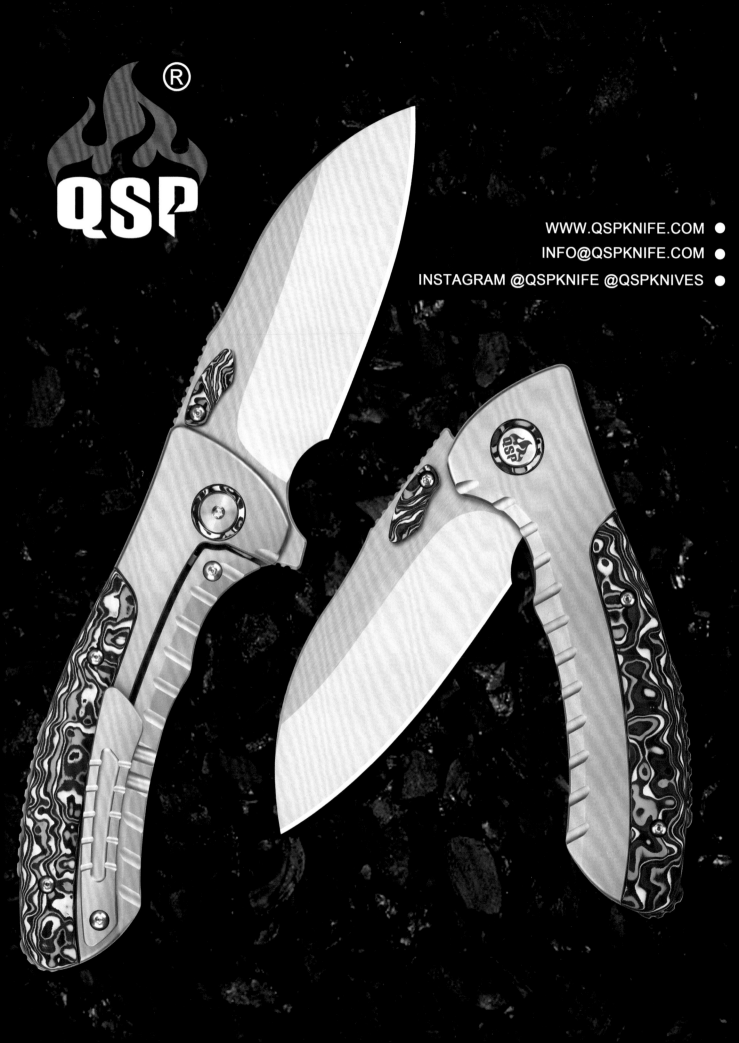

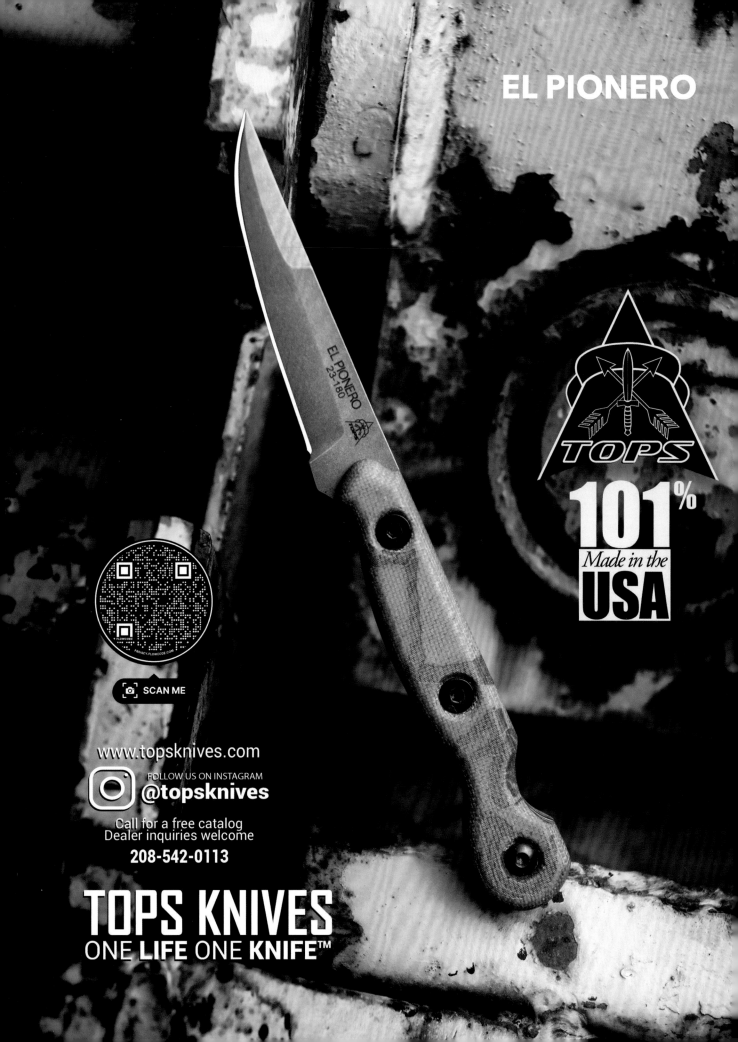

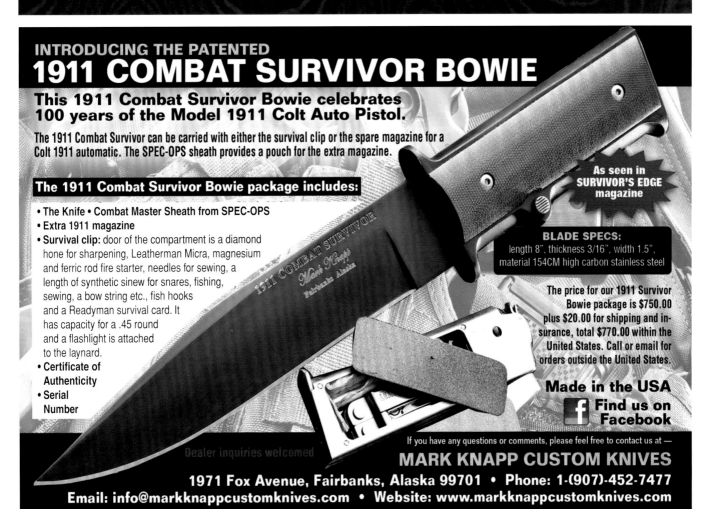

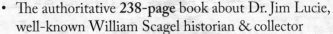
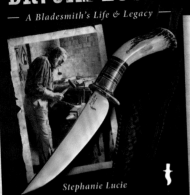
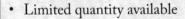

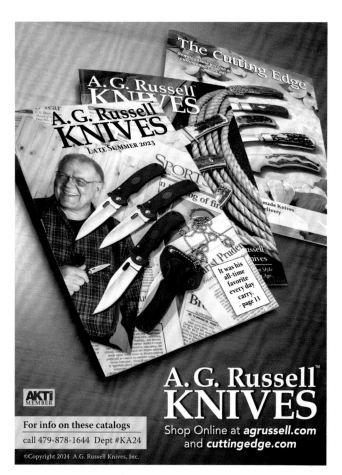
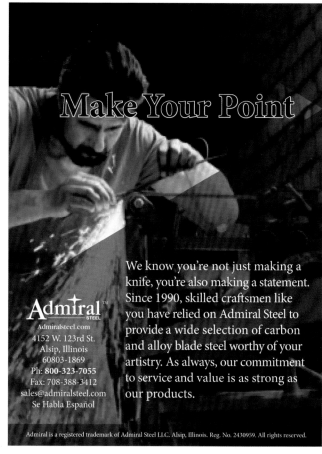
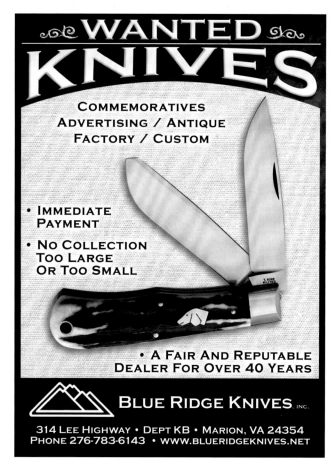

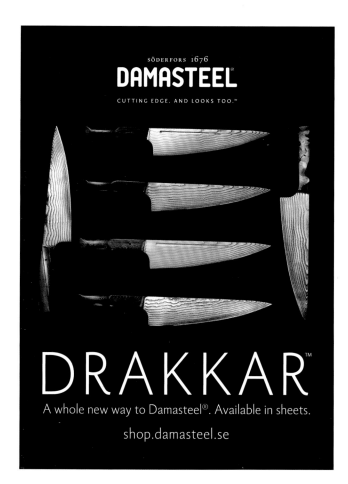

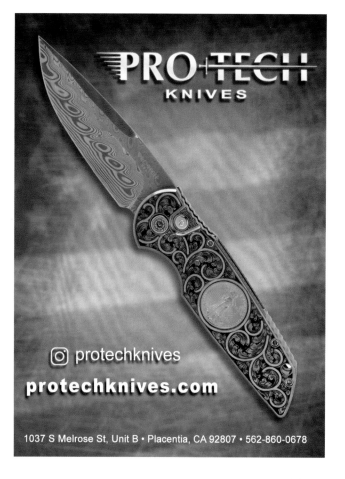

ENTER A NEW ERA

Military™ 2

Now featuring a
high-strength
Compression Lock®

🕷 **Spyderco**

spyderco.com   800 525 7770

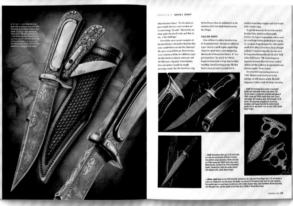

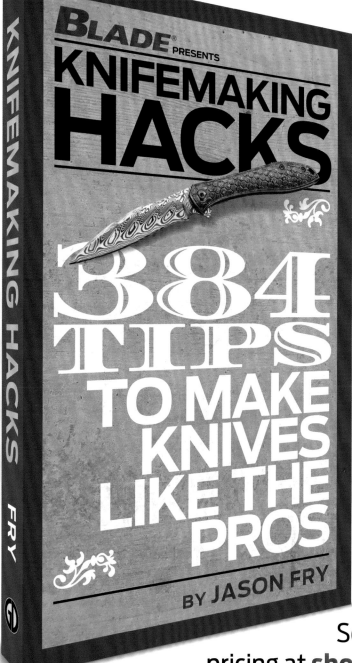

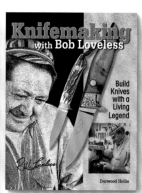

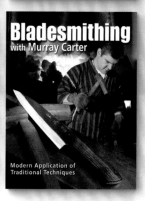

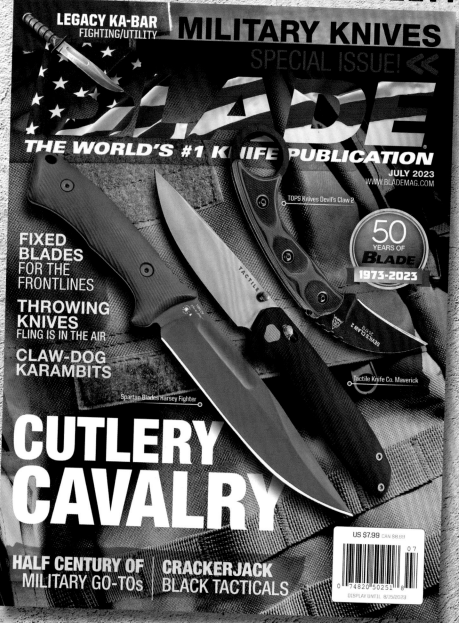